A Short History of Nova Scotia

Dr. Ed Whitcomb

From Sea to Sea Enterprises

Ottawa

Library and Archives Canada Cataloguing in Publication

Whitcomb, Dr. Edward A.
A Short History of Nova Scotia / Ed Whitcomb.

Includes bibliographical references and index.
ISBN 978-0-9694667-9-6

1. Nova Scotia – History. I. Title.

FC2311.W44 2009   971.6   C2009-902291-5

Printed in Canada by Dollco Printing, Ottawa

Table of Contents

Preface v

1. Early Beginnings, to 1713 1

2. France vs England, 1713-1763 5

3. Establishing a British Colony, 1763-1814 11

4. Responsible Government, 1814-1850 17

5. Railroads, Schools, and Confederation, 1850-1867 25

6. Anti-Confederation, 1867-1882 32

7. Liberal Forever, 1882-1914 37

8. War and Depression, 1914-1933 43

9. Angus L. Macdonald, 1933-1954 51

10. The Stanfield Years, 1954-1970 59

    Suggestions for Further Reading 67

    Index 68

This Book is Dedicated to the

people of Nova Scotia

Preface

This is the sixth in a series of history books on Canada's ten provinces. The idea for this series first arose in 1969 when I moved to Nova Scotia. Being new to the province and knowing very little about it, I went looking for a short history book which would provide an outline of the development of my newly-adopted home. There was no such book. In fact, there were hardly any short histories of any of Canada's provinces. In 1975 I decided to write the sort of book I had been looking for, and began with my native province of Manitoba. Over 8,000 copies of that *Short History of Manitoba* have been sold, which suggests that I was not alone in wanting good, short provincial histories. The project to write histories of all the provinces was delayed by family and career, but the Centennials of Alberta and Saskatchewan put the series back on track, and the short histories of those provinces were published in 2005. It made sense to continue with western and then central Canada so *British Columbia* was published in 2006 and *Ontario* in 2007. Now I have finally returned to the province that inspired the idea in the first place.

This *Short History of Nova Scotia* is designed to provide the average reader with a quick but accurate survey of the broad outline of Nova Scotia's development. The emphasis in this book is on the political developments that shaped the province as it is today, subjects such as the natives, immigration and settlement, economic activities such as the fishing, farming and mining, and the attainment of responsible government. It explains the serious shortcomings of the Confederation arrangements, developments before World War I, prohibition, and the long Depression of 1919-1939. World War II and the post-war developments complete the account.

Every historian has a point of view that determines which of the thousands of issues he or she will discuss, which of the millions of facts he or she will mention, and what things he or she will emphasize or ignore. This is essentially a political history, with some reference to economic and social developments, and it clearly emphasizes provincial rather than national or local issues. It seeks to explain Nova Scotia's side in disputes between the province and the federal government. It is not "popular history," and does not include pictures because there are several excellent picture books of Nova Scotia. While the achievements of Nova Scotians are documented, some criticisms are made of the heroes, politicians and groups who have shaped the province. In short, it is but one perspective on a very fascinating and complex society. My greatest hope is that this small book will encourage others to read more and to write more on the dozens of issues and perspectives necessary to obtain a full understanding of any society's development.

This account ends with the Stanfield government. Some readers will want it to cover more recent developments, but there is a point where history merges into political science or journalism. While we know the broad outline of recent events, we do not have access to Cabinet decisions, correspondence or the memoirs of most participants, and the secondary literature becomes less comprehensive. Many issues are still current, some still the subject of sharp debate, and many views on them are more subjective than objective. Much research has to be done and many books and articles written before the recent past falls into a proper historical perspective.

Many people helped with the preparation of this book. A number of professors, editors, analysts and experts read part or most of the text, and made many valuable corrections and suggestions. They include Dr. Jim Bickerton, Dr. R. Matthew Bray, Dr. Margaret Conrad, Dr. Stephen Henderson, Dr. Daniel Livermore, Margaret Poetschke, and Dr. David A. Sutherland. I alone am responsible for the weaknesses that remain in the book. The cover design and map were prepared by Linda Turenne using a Natural Resources Canada map and the colours of the official flag of Nova Scotia. Clifford Ford did the formatting and page layouts. John Colyer of Dellco Printers helped with the technical details. Most helpful of all was my wife, Kai, whose support and patience makes these books possible.

Ottawa, May, 2009.

Chapter One

Early Beginnings, to 1713

The history of Nova Scotia reflects the interplay of geography and people. The province juts out into the cold and stormy North Atlantic, and the sea has been as important as the land in shaping the province's history. It would be an island were it not for the narrow isthmus that connects it to North America. Indeed, Nova Scotia contains hundreds of islands including Cape Breton which constitutes a sixth of the province's area. With a land area of only 55,000 square kilometers it is both the second smallest and the second most densely populated of Canada's provinces and territories.

Stretching 500 kilometers from northeast to southwest, Nova Scotia's shoreline is over 6,000 kilometers long. No point in the province is more than 70 kilometers from the sea, and the vast majority of its people live within a few kilometers of the shore. Its major economic activities have centered on fishing, trading, shipbuilding, seafaring, smuggling, warfare, tourism, and off-shore oil and gas. For centuries Nova Scotia's interests and contacts lay across the sea, not with the rest of Canada.

Nova Scotia is part of the Appalachian mountain chain that runs along the east coast of North America from Georgia to Newfoundland. The province can be divided into three basic geographic areas or landscapes. Half of it consists of uplands running along the entire southeast coast from Cape Breton to Yarmouth. The area is based on granite bedrock, heavily scarred by glaciers, rugged and poorly drained, a land of forests, lakes, swamps, short rivers and very little agricultural land. This coast is heavily indented, dotted with hundreds of islands and small harbours. Many of the harbours became fishing villages – Louisbourg, Canso, Sheet Harbour, Lunenburg, Liverpool, Shelburne, and Yarmouth. Halifax-Bedford Basin is one of the largest harbours in the world.

To the northwest are lowlands which run almost the full length of the province. This swath of territory includes the Fundy Shore, the Annapolis Valley, the farmlands around Kentville and Truro, the Isthmus of Chignecto, the Northumberland coast from the New Brunswick border to the Strait of Canso, and the interior of Cape Breton around the Bras d'Or lakes. Part of it is rich farmland, part is mixed farmland, meadow and forest. The shorelines are straight, often lined with cliffs, with only a few good harbours such as Digby and Pictou. The valleys are gentle, slowly rising into hills with increasingly marginal farmland that gradually gives way to forest. This region includes the

Bay of Fundy, 200 kilometers long and 50 wide, where the highest tides in the world reach 17 meters. Most of the towns in this region are agricultural service centres such as Wolfville, Truro, Kentville, and Windsor.

A third geographical feature is the highlands. The most spectacular are the Cape Breton Highlands on the western half of the island, often rising in sheer cliffs and forming a plateau over 400 meters above sea level. West of the Strait of Canso are the Antigonish Highlands separating the lowlands of Northumberland from the uplands of Canso and the southeast coast. Farther west are the Chignecto Highlands separating the watersheds of the Northumberland shore and the Bay of Fundy. To the southwest, the Annapolis Valley is separated from the Bay of Fundy by the North Mountain range with a parallel range, the South Mountains, on the opposite side of the Valley. These areas are very lightly populated with the exception of the mining and industrial areas of Amherst, Springhill, and New Glasgow-Stellarton-Trenton.

Present-day Nova Scotia was discovered, explored, and settled by peoples who came from Asia over 10,000 years ago. The Mi'kmaq who settled Nova Scotia belonged to the Algonkian language group which stretches from the Rocky Mountains to the Atlantic. They were a semi-nomadic people, hunting moose, caribou, and beaver during the winter and then migrating to the coast to fish for salmon, cod, seals, and whales, to hunt ducks and geese, and to gather oysters and clams. They mastered the rugged geography and inhospitable climate with birch bark canoes, snow shoes, fur clothes, and implements made of wood, clay, stone, and bone.

The Mi'kmaq had well-established social organizations, assembling in large numbers in the summer while dispersing into smaller groups in winter. They believed that spirits lived in all objects, be they humans, animals, trees, or rocks. They had family units, but divorce was common and polygamy was practiced. European settlement along fertile valleys gradually pushed the aboriginal peoples farther and farther into the interior. In the centuries of warfare between the English and the French, the natives allied with the latter. When France lost, the Mi'kmaq had to make peace with the English. Vastly outnumbered and overwhelmed, the M'kmaq were slowly relegated to dozens of small, uneconomic reserves, limited in their rights, and forced into dependency on government which violated the spirit if not the word of their treaties.

Leif Erickson may have been the first European to see Nova Scotia during his famous voyage of 1000 AD. John Cabot and his son, Sebastian, probably discovered it in 1497 or 1498. It is certain, however, that the Cabots confirmed the existence of the Atlantic cod fishery, one of the richest food supplies in the world. Soon, hundreds of fishing boats were crossing the Atlantic every year, exploring the coastline, and trading with the natives. Jacques Cartier explored the northern coastline of Nova Scotia in his 1534 voyage to the Gulf of St. Lawrence. During the summer the fishermen went ashore to dry their fish especially at Canso, which was one of the most important communities in the area for more than two centuries.

In 1604 the King of France establish a colony in the land they called L'Acadie or today's Maritime Provinces. Pierre du Guast, Sieur de Monts brought over 100 colonists to build a base at the mouth of the St. Croix River in present-day New Brunswick. Most of the settlers died, and the survivors moved across the Bay of Fundy to found Port Royal at the mouth of the Annapolis River. That site was easily defended, had good agricultural land and was close to friendly natives. Port Royal became the first site in Canada to be permanently inhabited by Europeans.

Not to be outdone, the King of England granted the same area to the London and Plymouth Company in 1606. When that company failed to develop the colony, England granted it to Sir William Alexander who named it New Scotland. The grant was written in Latin so the name was spelled Nova Scotia. Over the next century Nova Scotia remained overwhelmingly native with a French population of only 400 by 1650. One of the major successes of the French was converting the Mi'kmaq to Christianity, and relations between French and natives were cordial and mutually advantageous.

From time to time, additional groups of settlers were sent out from France, especially in the 1630s. The population expanded rapidly due mainly to little disease and extremely high marriage and birth rates. Settlements spread along the Annapolis Valley and up the rivers that flowed into the Bay of Fundy, to Grand Pré, Minas Basin, the shores of Chignecto Bay, and southwest to Pubnico. The Acadians developed a method of claiming farmland from the sea. They built dykes to keep out the tides, drained the salt water marshes, waited while the rains leached the salt out of the soil, and then grew wheat and hay on the rich land. Agriculture was supplemented by fishing, hunting and trading with the natives.

For decades the Acadians developed their communities virtually without government assistance or control. Society was close-knit and self-reliant, based on family, community, and the Catholic religion. The people had a simplistic, almost self-sufficient economy though they traded with New England and later with Louisbourg. France, however, had spent some effort and capital establishing Acadia to help protect its North American interests, and it saw the Acadian settlements as proof of territorial occupation and a source of militia and supplies during warfare. This threatened the English, who attacked Acadia whenever there was war with France. As wars became more frequent and substantial, the situation of the Acadians deteriorated. In its first century Port Royal passed back and forth between France and England ten times, the usual pattern being conquest by England and restoration to France in the peace treaties. The pattern began in 1613 with the first conquest by English colonists from Virginia.

One reason for French neglect was that Acadia was not as important to France as the Newfoundland fishery or the colony on the St. Lawrence. England's interest centered on competition with France for the fishery and on New England to the south, and English attacks on Port Royal were largely a response to pressure from colonists in New England. France's hold on the region was also weakened by the government's practice of dividing authority. In the 1630s a virtual civil war broke out between the forces of Menou d'Aulnay and Charles de LaTour, two strong-willed and ambitious soldiers who hated each other passionately. While peace treaties confirmed France's legal sovereignty over Nova Scotia, its actual control was very tenuous. France could not, for example, prevent New Englanders from landing on deserted beaches to dry their fish.

In 1689 the War of the League of Augsburg (King William's War) broke out between England and France. A year later New Englanders under Sir William Phips seized and sacked Port Royal. The Treaty of Ryswick of 1697 then returned the colony to France. Raids on Acadia and French attacks on New England ships resumed with the outbreak of the War of Spanish Succession (Queen Anne's War, 1701-1714). Acadian settlements on the Bay of Fundy and Minas Basin were destroyed, but Port Royal held out. By 1710 both the New Englanders and the British government had decided to eradicate the threat once and for all. On September 24 a force of 3,000 men under Colonel Francis Nicholson laid siege to Port Royal and a week later it capitulated. It was renamed Annapolis Royal after the English Queen. Three years later the Treaty of Utrecht finally transferred peninsular Nova Scotia to England. There would be disputes over the northern and eastern borders, but Port Royal and the Annapolis Valley Acadians would never again live under French sovereignty.

Chapter Two

France vs. England, 1713-1763

For over half a century France and England fought for supremacy over North America. The ink was hardly dry on the Treaty of Utrecht before both countries began planning the next stages in the struggle. By that Treaty France lost Acadia to England with the exceptions of Île St. Jean (Prince Edward Island) and Île Royale (Cape Breton). The exact borders of Acadia were not, however, clear.

France soon developed a strategy for preserving its North American possessions. It would develop Île Royale to protect the Atlantic fishery and the colony of New France. A massive fortress would guard the entrance to the St. Lawrence. The Isthmus of Chignecto and the Northumberland coast up to Canso would constitute a ring of defence for Île Royale. The Acadians in the Annapolis Valley were given one year to move to French-controlled territory or remain as British subjects. Aware of the poor soil on Île Royale, they chose to stay.

The British were far less certain of their strategy. Controlling a major part of the Atlantic fishery was a key goal. Protecting the American colonies was a priority because New England viewed France as a major threat. Anglo-French rivalries in India and the West Indies were important considerations, and London had to make concessions to the aspirations of its European allies. That mix of strategic priorities produced confusion and indifference to the fate of Nova Scotia.

Britain changed the name of Port Royal to Annapolis Royal, but British authority hardly extended beyond the walls of the fort. Since the French considered Canso outside the borders of Acadia, they retained possession of that vital port, and the British had to force them out in the early 1720s. No serious attempt was made by England to settle Acadia so it remained a colony of French Catholics. Successive British governors sought solutions, support, and advice from England only to be answered by silence or unenforceable instructions.

Meanwhile, France began constructing the huge fortress of Louisbourg, named for King Louis XV. When he saw the bills he is reported to have asked if the streets were paved with gold. The French chose English Harbour, a splendid site midway along the east coast. The site jutted out into the ocean, with the harbour to the north, Gabarus Bay to the south and an impenetrable marsh to the west.

Louisbourg became the greatest metropolis north of Boston. The fort consisted of a massive edifice of bastions, ramparts, walls, and emplacements for hundreds of canons. The port became one of the busiest in North America with a population of 3,000 by 1744. It contained stores, hotels, inns, churches, hospitals, schools, a theatre, and well-planned public spaces. It was the centre of one of the largest fisheries in the Atlantic, and its exports of fish vastly exceeded the value of the fur trade of New France. The fortress succeeded in impressing the Mi'kmaq, and they remained allied to France to the end of the wars.

At Annapolis Royal Lieutenant Governor Lawrence Armstrong drafted a constitution, established some courts, and issued some laws and regulations. Britain could not decide whether the capital should be in Annapolis Royal, the centre of population, or at Canso. The small population of New Englanders demanded an Assembly, but successive governors delayed calling one because the New Englanders' interests clashed with Britain's.

The final contest for empire between Britain and France took place in two phases, known in European history as the War of Austrian Succession, 1744-1748, and the Seven Years' War, 1756-63. The British were not prepared for this war but the New Englanders were. In wartime the French attacked their ports and shipping, and encouraged native attacks on the New England frontier. The French were competitors for the Atlantic fishery and Atlantic trade. Besides that, the French were foreigners and Catholics, and the Acadians occupied valuable land. These factors left the New Englanders in no doubt as to the rightness of their cause or the certainty of its outcome. Governor William Shirley of Massachusetts raised a colonial militia. London sent a fleet with 3,500 men to help them. On 30 April 1745 William Pepperrell landed over 4,000 troops at Gabarus Bay. The colonial militia dragged their cannon through the swamp which the French thought impenetrable and began bombarding the fortress, the town and the harbour.

Having spent vast sums of money building the fortress, Paris seemingly lost interest in it, allowing corrupt administrators to pocket the money that should have gone for supplies, salaries and maintenance. By the late 1740s the 1,400 troops were poorly fed, clothed and housed, underpaid and bordering on mutiny under the incompetent Governor, Dupont du Chambon.

The New Englanders launched a series of bloody attacks on the fortress. When they failed, morale began to sag. Finally they concentrated their guns on the Island Battery at the mouth of the harbour and overwhelmed it. From that position they concentrated their firepower on the main fortress and Louisbourg capitulated on 17 June 1745. The following year France sent a massive fleet of

31 ships and 7,000 men to recapture the fortress. Decimated by disease, incompetence, bad luck and terrible timing the fleet sailed back to France without firing a shot. In the negotiations for the Treaty of Aix-la-Chapelle of 1748 France was adamant that it would keep Île Royale. England's overall interests were served by its gains in other areas so it returned Île Royale to France to the extreme annoyance of the New Englanders.

France immediately began rebuilding Louisbourg and asserting control over the Isthmus of Chignecto. In 1749 it built a fort at Beauséjour just west of the present border with New Brunswick. The British sent Lieutenant-Colonel Charles Lawrence to build a fort, which he modestly named after himself, on the south side of the river facing Fort Beauséjour. The French used the Mi'kmaq to attack British positions and settlements and the growing viciousness of frontier fighting strengthened the resolve of both sides to fight to the finish.

England finally decided to make a huge investment in its North American colonies by matching the investment Paris had made in Louisbourg. Britain decided to create a fort to anchor English settlement in Nova Scotia and to provide a capital for its neglected province. It decided to attract English Protestant settlers who would gradually outnumber the Acadians. The site chosen was the Bay of Chebucto, the best port in Nova Scotia, easily defended from a large hill and from islands in the mouth of the harbor. It was named after the responsible British minister, George Montagu-Dunk, Earl of Halifax.

London appointed Edward Cornwallis to found the new community. On 21 June 1749 he arrived with 2,500 settlers, a mixed group of English, Scottish, and Irish workers, carpenters, masons, merchants, preachers, and doctors. In the first winter, many died from poor diet, poor housing, disease and drunkenness. These settlers built a fort, a neatly-laid out town, and English Canada's first church, St Paul's. Here Canada's first newspaper was published in 1752. Halifax was a naval base with no agricultural hinterland, and for centuries it prospered during wartime and struggled to survive in periods of peace. It also struggled in the first years against repeated attacks by France's Mi'kmaq allies.

In 1750 a new wave of immigrants arrived. These were New Englanders born and raised in the colonies, hard-working, deeply religious, and not particularly patriotic but eager to grow rich filling the demands of the Royal Navy for supplies and the demands of its sailors for dark rum, cheap entertainment and loose women. The New Englanders had left free-wheeling, self-governing colonies where rebellion against British rule was brewing for an autocratic military base run by arrogant officers they regarded as incompetent. Like the Acadians they saw nothing wrong in selling supplies to both sides, and infuriated British officials could do little to stop them.

The British elite in turn regarded the New Englanders as disrespectful, disloyal, dishonest, undisciplined and greedy. The two groups soon clashed over the New Englanders' demand for an elected Assembly, which they would control, and the elite's desire to exercise complete control in the interests of the British Empire and, of course, of themselves. The governors procrastinated, knowing that an Assembly would challenge the nepotism, corruption, and inefficiency that characterized their administrations.

The war with France and the desire to attract more New Englanders changed London's thinking and in 1758 Governor Lawrence was ordered to call elections. On 2 October 1758 the first elected Assembly in what is now Canada met in Halifax. Gradually the Assembly asserted some control over spending and it became somewhat of a check on the power of the governor and his Executive Council. In the same year the government established the county system as the basis for local government and provincial elections. The original counties included Halifax, Lunenburg, Annapolis, Kings, and Cumberland, with Hants and Windsor soon following. That system remains essentially in effect to this day, one later change being the establishment of townships.

British policy towards the Acadians was to overwhelm and assimilate them into English Protestant society. Britain planned to settle large groups of Protestants amongst the Acadians. There was no great incentive for people to leave the British Isles, however, and New Englanders were dissuaded from migrating by French power. Britain therefore recruited several thousand German, Swiss, and French Protestants as settlers. They arrived in Halifax between 1750 and 1752, and after several miserable winters they were settled in Lunenburg. They eventually specialized in fishing, seafaring and shipbuilding, occupations that made them famous.

In 1754, the British began planning the systematic destruction of New France. In the spring of 1755, Britain sent 2,000 colonial militia and 500 regulars to face the 200 regulars and Acadian militia and Mi'kmaq in Fort Beauséjour. The British attacked on June 13 and three days later the fort capitulated. Governor Lawrence was furious with the fact that hundreds of Acadians had been fighting for France.

In 1713 Britain inherited around 2,000 Acadians along the Fundy shore. By 1730 that population had grown to 2,500 and to 10,000 by 1750, concentrated in the Annapolis Valley but stretching well past Yarmouth, north to the Minas Basin, around Chignecto Bay into present-day New Brunswick, and along the Northumberland shore. The Acadians had never been particularly supportive of France, and were determined to remain neutral in any wars between France and

England. Britain lacked the power to govern them but it did demand that they swear an oath of allegiance to the British crown. The French Government regarded the Acadians as assets in the wars with England, and French priests urged them not to take the oath. In fact, many Acadians did take an oath of loyalty but made it conditional on exemption from service in the militia.

For 40 years British governors tried to convince the Acadians to swear unconditional oaths of allegiance. By 1755 Governor Cornwallis was determined to obtain a guarantee of their neutrality, and he told them to sign an unconditional oath or else. Again they refused. Cornwallis' successor, Governor Charles Lawrence, decided to deal with the issue once and for all, and this time he had the power to enforce the threat. Lawrence assumed that the Acadians understood that and would sign the oath. But he was mistaken, for once more they refused. Several weeks later they refused again, thinking the threats were as hollow as previous ones. This time they too were mistaken.

These misjudgments on both sides precipitated one of the greatest tragedies in Canadian history. Upon receiving another refusal to take the oath, Lawrence concluded that the Acadians had clearly opted for France. In 1755 he sent Lieutenant Colonel John Winslow to Grand Pré to begin deporting them to other British colonies. Up and down the Bay of Fundy some 7,000 Acadians were rounded up, often without sufficient time to collect possessions. Some were hunted down in the forests where they sought refuge, and more were deported in the following years. The English did not deliberately break up families, but in their haste they did not ensure that families stayed together.

The deportation scene was one of confused and disorientated adults carrying their young and elderly onto ships, of husbands, wives, and children crying out for each other against a backdrop of burning houses, barns, churches, and crops. At sea many died of disease or drowning. Many were landed in colonies along the American coast against the will of the inhabitants, where they spent the rest of their lives in isolation, poverty, and misery. Others were sent to the West Indies or France. Their suffering was captured forever in the epic poem *Evangeline* by Henry Wadsworth Longfellow.

Many Acadians were assimilated into the majority English populations thus fulfilling one of the objectives of their deportation. But many others settled in groups and kept their identity, the most famous being the settlers in the French colony of Louisiana where the name Acadian evolved into Cajun. In Nova Scotia perhaps a third of them fled north and west into the unpopulated areas of present-day New Brunswick, the Northumberland shore, Prince Edward Island, and Cape Breton. Many of those deported gradually returned to join them. In spite of the deportation the Acadians remained a nation in the proper sense of the word, a people with a common identity based on ethnicity, culture, language, and history, an identity separate from that of their sister nation, the French Canadians of Quebec. In the Maritimes the British attempt at assimilation backfired because surviving the "Grand Deportation" became the central unifying theme in the Acadian national identity.

The expulsion of the Acadians did achieve its strategic goals. It removed the potential threat to the British position in Nova Scotia, and it ended the supply of militia and food to Louisbourg. The next element of British strategy was to bring overwhelming power to bear on that fortress. Under General Jeffrey Amherst, 13,000 sailors and 13,000 soldiers were assembled in Halifax along with a fleet of 40 ships. This time the French defences contained 3,500 soldiers, 3,500 sailors, strengthened fortifications, plenty of provisions, high morale, and a competent Governor, Chevalier de Drucour.

On June 8 the British landed at Gabaras Bay and pushed the French infantry back. The French may have made a tactical mistake by not counterattacking before the bulk of the British force landed. Instead, they withdrew behind their fortifications and held the British off in weeks of intensive battle. The French position was strengthened by the presence of four huge battleships in the harbor. Finally relentless shelling set fire to two of the French ships, another was attacked and set on fire, and the fourth was captured. The English ships could then enter the harbour and fire directly on the fortress. Governor Drucour surrendered on July 26. His only goal had been to hold out long enough to prevent the British from attacking Quebec that summer, and he achieved that goal. France's goals, however, were to hold Louisbourg, Île Royale, and New France, and it lost them all in the Treaty of Paris of 1763. From that date forward the whole of Nova Scotia would be British.

Chapter Three

Establishing a British Colony, 1763-1814

The Treaty of Paris ended the Seven Years' War. In the subsequent negotiations France's main goal was to maintain a base for the Atlantic fishery. This it did with the retention of Saint Pierre and Miquelon off the coast of Newfoundland. Britain gained the rest of Acadia including Cape Breton and New France which it renamed Quebec. Acquiring Quebec may have been a strategic blunder because that removed the French threat to the 13 English colonies which had made them dependent on England for defence. Twelve years later, their successful revolt produced a wave of the Loyalist immigration to Nova Scotia, with profound effects on Atlantic Canada.

The Treaty of Paris transferred Île Royale and Île St. Jean to Nova Scotia where they were renamed Cape Breton and St. John's Island respectively. Britain now controlled all of the Maritimes and the entire area was governed from Halifax for the first time in its history. The fortress at Louisbourg was destroyed leaving a poor struggling fishing village in its wake. With the end of military activities the population of Halifax declined from 5,000 to 1,500 miserable souls fighting over the few remaining jobs. The colonial government went heavily in debt to maintain a higher level of spending than was justified in peacetime. In 1769 St. John's Island became a separate colony eventually renamed Prince Edward Island or PEI, never to be reunited to Nova Scotia.

Even before the war had ended the demographic makeup of the province changed dramatically. With the French threat removed, New Englanders known as Planters flooded into the Annapolis Valley, up to Minas Bay and around the Bay of Chignecto. These immigrants were successful at farming, fishing, lumbering, and commerce and had money, equipment and trading connections in New England. Many had also abandoned Anglicanism for the new dissenting Protestant religions. Numbering some 8,000 they pushed the overall population of the colony to 13,000. Some New England fishermen decided to establish new ports, and Liverpool and Yarmouth sprang up. At the same time, Acadians who had fled northwest to the forests began trickling back to the lands not occupied by the Planters. Some also congregated in Cape Breton villages such as Arichat and Cheticamp where poor soil forced them to concentrate on fishing.

Then Scots began settling along the Northumberland shore, starting at Pictou in 1773 and spreading east to Antigonish and Cape Breton. At last the province was receiving settlers who gave its name real meaning, and by 1803 some 17,000 Scots had come. Those in Pictou and to the west were mainly

Protestant, those settling to the east were mainly Gaelic-speaking Roman Catholic Highlanders. The landscape, soil, and climate were similar to those of Scotland where conditions had produced a sturdy sense of self-sufficiency. Their goal was to establish peaceful and prosperous homes and villages. Unlike the New Englanders, Scots cared little about elected government or what it could do for them, making them ideal citizens in the eyes of the Halifax elite.

Soon a trickle of Ulstermen began to arrive, English-speaking Presbyterian Lowland Scots from Northern Ireland. They came as individuals rather than clans or groups, settled mainly in central Nova Scotia, and were easily assimilated into a more English culture. Some of these settlers pushed the Mi'kmaq off their lands and farther into poverty, dependence, and hopelessness. Poor Irish Catholics also began to migrate, settling mainly in Halifax. By 1775 the province's population had grown to over 20,000, roughly two-thirds from New England, 2,000 of them living in Halifax.

Competent governance emerged very slowly. The Assembly was dominated by Halifax merchants whose interests lay in squeezing every possible penny out of the British government and navy. Clashes soon arose between the elected Assembly and the appointed Executive Council. A series of weak or uninterested governors meant that power was wielded by the cabal of Halifax merchants who controlled the Council. Chief among them was Joshua Mauger who had grown rich manufacturing rum for thirsty British troops. He ensured that the tariff on imported spirits was so high that virtually none was imported, which sharply reduced customs revenue. When Governor William Campbell tried to lower the tariff, Mauger used his influence in London to have Campbell removed. Governor Francis Legge, who arrived in 1773, had little more success when his goals clashed with those of the elite who used their positions to pocket inflated incomes in the form of fees and outright corruption.

Local governance also remained feeble. All municipal administrators were appointed by the governor from amongst the friends and relatives of the elite. The Halifax merchants controlled both provincial and local governments for generations, stunting the development of democracy, good governance and the economy. Throughout the province people grew accustomed to asking Halifax for government services rather than raising taxes locally, a practice that bred corruption, irresponsibility and a sense of dependency.

Halifax was saved from its political, economic, cultural, and even moral degeneration by the outbreak of the American War of Independence in 1775. There was no danger of Nova Scotia joining the rebellion because of pro-British sentiment, the British fleet, the rush of spending on every product the province could produce, and the presence of European settlers and Acadians with no interest in American politics. American privateers also made the mistake of attacking Nova Scotian ships and settlements. In general Nova Scotians did not see it as their war and few volunteered to fight the American rebels.

The war itself hardly touched the province except for the raids of American privateers in the early years. The Treaty of Paris of 1783 did not affect the borders of present-day Nova Scotia, but the American victory transformed Nova Scotia forever. A portion of the American population had sympathized with Britain, and thousands had fought on the British side. When Britain lost the war they became refugees. Around 35,000 Loyalists came to Nova Scotia, 14,000 of them to the west side of the Bay of Fundy. While most were British in origin, some were German, Dutch or Irish, and more than 3,000 were Blacks. They came from all classes, all trades and all professions. Some were rich but most were destitute. They needed complete support – housing, food, free land, implements, and welfare to get them through the first few years. They also brought the strongly-held view that having sacrificed everything for the British cause Britain now owed them appointment to virtually every government job even if that meant dismissing incumbents. That attitude would poison relations between them and the rest of the population for decades.

In the winter and spring of 1782-83, ten thousand Loyalists arrived in Halifax where they overwhelmed the local administration. Many were housed in churches, tents, and makeshift huts, with inadequate food, clothing, and sanitation. Presiding over the chaos was the new governor, John Parr. His career as a tough, hard-drinking officer accustomed to obedience left him unsuited for the challenges of the next decade. Parr sent thousands of refugees to Shelburne on the south coast, which exploded from a tiny village to a town of 8,000 within months. It had no agricultural hinterland, and within a few years almost all the new inhabitants had moved on. The government was slow to survey and allocate free land, and bribery soon became a standard practice for obtaining land or supplies. The government grew more corrupt as it struggled to deal with an increasingly embittered populace. Many Loyalists simply squatted on vacant land or pushed natives off their land, and then waited impatiently for an official deed.

A clear division quickly emerged between the newcomers and the earlier immigrants or "old comers." The latter were divided in two groups, the New England Planters, who did not share many of the Loyalists' attitudes, and the governing elite. The Loyalists believed that they should be in charge rather than the officials who had enriched themselves off the war instead of fighting it. On the east side of the Bay of Fundy the Loyalists demanded independence from Halifax. London agreed, and in 1784 New Brunswick was established as a separate colony, a severe blow to the power, wealth, and pride of Halifax.

Cape Breton was made a separate colony under the inept, intransigent, and quarrelsome Lieutenant-Governor Joseph Frederick Wallet DesBarres. Sydney was mapped out as the grandiose capital, and a trickle of Loyalists arrived. Its forests were reserved for the Royal Navy, however, and coal mining was discouraged to protect industry in Great Britain. While the Scots struggled to establish their homesteads and the Acadians kept to themselves, the Loyalists fought over scarce government jobs in the stagnant economy.

In the scramble for land, supplies, and jobs, the Loyalists cheated and fought with each other. The ones who suffered the most were the Black Loyalists. They had been promised the same compensation as white Loyalists, but reality was very different. They were given smaller grants of inferior land and less food and provisions. Denied the vote and equality before the law almost half of them migrated to West Africa. The remainder struggled on for many decades against discrimination, the inescapable poverty resulting from their inferior land grants, and barriers to movement, education and employment.

Over the next decade Nova Scotia struggled to absorb the Loyalists. Time and death solved some of the problems, and many Loyalists left in frustration. But for many a sense of grievance remained, of unfulfilled promises, of being tricked by false propaganda about the wonders of their new wilderness homes, and especially of not receiving the positions they felt were their due. They received little sympathy from the "old comers", partly because of their endless complaining even when they received privileges.

One notable privilege was the status of the Anglican Church of England. The British Government believed that weak religious principles were one of the underlying causes of the American revolt, and was determined to provide better moral leadership in the remaining British colonies. The Anglican Church was given a privileged position in society and government, and its salaries, buildings, and expenses were subsidized. The first college in the province was King's College, established in Windsor in 1789, government-supported but open only to Anglicans. Favouritism towards Anglicans caused serious religious, social, political, legal and educational problems for a century. The attempt to create an established church failed partly because its clergy looked to the church for what it could do for them, and more and more Anglicans joined the evangelical Protestant faiths.

The Loyalists were soon well represented in the Assembly where they battled with the "old comers." Within years government became virtually paralyzed because of their differences and battles between the Assembly and the governor. This paralysis ended in 1792 with the appointment of John Wentworth as governor, a position he held through 16 stormy years. Wentworth, Nova Scotia's first civilian governor, had been a successful governor of New

population. Ethnically the Irish were the largest group of Catholics, followed closely by the Scots, then Acadians and a small minority of Mi'kmaq. The two largest Protestant denominations were the Methodists and the Baptists, followed by the Presbyterians. In 1925 the Methodists and most Presbyterians combined to form the United Church of Canada, now the largest Protestant religion in the province with 16% of the population. Anglicans account for 13%, Baptists for 10%, and Presbyterians for 2.5%.

Though all these denominations were Christian, religion was a divisive force in Nova Scotian history. The privileged position of the Anglican Church caused bitter political strife. Congregations were segregated within individual churches, the rich sitting at the front, the poor near the back. Blacks eventually grew tired of segregation and established their own churches. Congregations were told that their religion was better than others and that others were a threat to them. Animosity, hate and distrust abounded, and religion affected politics and society at every level - schools, business contracts, employment, and the selection of juries and hence of crime and punishment.

Physical battles between religious groups were common. Religious fervour was so intense that fights broke out within congregations, the most famous occurring among Presbyterians in Pictou in 1830. The sheriff erected a fence ten feet high to separate the two factions, but one man was killed and scores injured in the riot. Churches also intervened openly and forcefully in politics. In the late 1840s Catholics constituted one third the population of Halifax but held only one fifteenth of the positions in government. In the 1847 election the clergy urged all Catholics to vote Liberal to correct that imbalance; the Baptist Church then urged its followers to vote Conservative.

Religion also made education extremely contentious. King's College in Windsor was founded in 1789 as a government-funded college open only to Anglicans. Dalhousie College began as a non-denominational college with government support but soon came under the influence of the Presbyterians. Other denominations founded colleges and requested government support, the Baptists for Acadia College in Wolfville and the Catholics for St. Mary's in Halifax and St. Francis Xavier in Antigonish.

During this period the future of Cape Breton was decided. As an independent colony after 1784 it was a spectacular failure. It had no geographic unity and the rugged terrain precluded any internal communications system. Because of British economic policy neither the coal resources nor the forests could be developed, and few immigrants came because there was little good agricultural land. In Sydney a small coterie of would-be grandees fought over the limited spoils of office. The governors were duty bound to establish an Assembly but the overwhelming majority of Catholics could not vote or hold office. The governors therefore ruled by proclamation rather than by laws passed by an Assembly.

The question of taxing rum decided the fate of Cape Breton. Two citizens decided to challenge the tax on imported rum on the grounds that only an elected Assembly could approve such a tax. The courts agreed. The British Government was faced with a choice: create an Assembly to make the taxes legal or reunite Cape Breton to Nova Scotia. On 1 January 1820 Cape Breton was reunited to Nova Scotia, thereby settling the last of the territorial boundaries. One outraged citizen described the arrangement as a "jewel in a hog's snout." The dispossessed Sydney elite got over its outrage and the indifferent Scots and Acadians gradually adopted a sense of regionalism that endures to this day as a significant factor in the Nova Scotia's identity.

The union of the two colonies then produced one of the most significant advances for democracy in Nova Scotia. Cape Breton was entitled to two MLAs in the Assembly in Halifax. Catholics had been excluded from office by the oath of allegiance, but allowing two Protestants to represent them would be unjust. The Assembly unanimously voted to change the oath, and in 1822 Lawrence Kavanaugh became the first elected Catholic politician in the province.

In the two decades after 1830 politics was dominated by the struggle to create better governance. Power was concentrated in the hands of the appointed governor who ruled through a small Executive Council which he appointed. They appointed a number of administrators who managed municipal governments, courts, police, and customs collection. This system allowed a small elite to take excessive advantage of its power. They granted themselves huge salaries, collected large fees for minor services, held their offices for life, hired each others' relatives and friends, did not properly account for funds, and reinforced their power with the full force of the law and courts. The elite, who came to be known as Tories, consisted of the richest men in Halifax, and at one time six of the nine Councilors sat on the Board of Directors of the only bank in the province.

One example of their abuse was the practice of exempting their own property from taxation. Another was using prisoners to produce goods for their companies. The mansions they built stood in sharp contrast to the slums of the poor where disease swept hundreds to premature deaths. While the population of Halifax groaned under the weight of excessive taxation and fees, services such as roads, sewers, clean water, cemeteries, sidewalks, and hospitals were virtually non-existent.

The elected Assembly was designed to give voice to the popular will. No law could be passed without the Assembly's approval, but proclamations and regulations could, providing considerable scope to avoid the Assembly. No taxes could be raised without its approval, but fees could be charged for services. The biggest source of revenue was customs, and that was controlled by Britain. The Assembly itself was mainly composed of lawyers from Halifax who were also members of the elite.

In the 1820s a number of MLAs, journalists, and prominent citizens began criticizing these abuses. They founded the Mechanics' Institute, the Temperance Society and the Nova Scotian Philanthropic Society to promote education, learning, new ideas, better living conditions, better morals, and patriotism. One of them was the judge and author Thomas Chandler Haliburton, creator of the famous *Sam Slick* sketches. Politically these people came to be known as Reformers. One of their leaders, Jothan Blanchard, editor of the *Colonial Patriot* in Pictou, may have influenced Joseph Howe, owner and editor of the *Novascotian,* to join their cause. Howe started criticizing the abuses in the *Novascotian* and publishing court proceedings and Assembly speeches that threw light on government incompetence and abuse.

The government reacted to the growing chorus of criticism by attacking the critics. On New Year's Day 1835 Howe published an anonymous letter specifically charging certain magistrates with pocketing thousands of dollars of taxpayers' money without providing services to justify the expenses. The government had two choices: ignore the challenge and in effect admit guilt or charge Howe with criminal libel and hopefully end his attacks. They chose to charge him. His article was, in fact, libelous and lawyers told him he had no chance of winning the case.

Howe decided to defend himself. In a six-hour speech he established a reputation as a great orator, an amazing feat as he had not often spoken in public and was not a lawyer. He argued that his articles could not lead to public unrest because exposing government graft would improve governance and therefore produce a more complacent public. The jury took ten minutes to reach a judgment – innocent!

It was a landmark decision in the history of British North America. Prior to that, the Assembly was virtually the only check on the government. Now Howe had established that the press could expose corruption without facing jail through a court system stacked with government appointees. The British government sent new instructions to Governor Sir Colin Campbell stating that there could be no favouritism towards the Anglican Church, that the

Chief Justice could not be on the Executive Council, and that no single commercial sector such as banking could have more than one representative on the Council.

In 1837 Howe was elected to the Assembly where he quickly became the leader of the Reformers. To promote his paper Howe had travelled all over the province – he knew it like no other politician and the people knew and loved him. He was smart, hard-working, widely-read, well-prepared, witty, clear, devastating in his criticisms, and attuned to his audiences. He was, however, a flawed politician and leader. Though his contributions were outstanding, he joined the movements for responsible government and the repeal of Confederation after they had been launched by others. Intemperate remarks and fights with Catholics and Baptists cost him the respect of many, lead to one duel and postponed and then limited his tenure as premier.

One of the first victories of Howe and the Reformers was the incorporation of Halifax as a city with an elected government. As a result, corruption was reduced and improvements to infrastructure began to appear. In the Assembly Howe kept up his attacks on the corruption of officials, and on privileges such as those of the Anglican Church. His campaign included speeches, editorials, letters and addresses to the government in London.

While Howe and his colleagues knew that government was not functioning properly, they were not sure how to fix it. Originally all they wanted was to eradicate the abuse in the existing system by having better people appointed and acquiring better accounting procedures. Britain knew that the system had to be improved, but did not know the solutions either. As a partial response London created a third institution, the Legislative Council. It was the equivalent of the modern Canadian Senate, an appointed body of advisers who could provide a second opinion on government actions in addition to that of the Assembly. That reform did not end the problems.

The situation was far worse in Upper and Lower Canada where armed rebellion erupted. In response, London sent Lord Durham to propose solutions for all the British North American colonies. Durham's conclusion was that the underlying flaw in the system was the fact that the Executive Council was responsible to London but much of its revenue came from the Assembly, and it could not always satisfy the interests of both. Clashes with the Assembly over spending, appointments and other government matters would continue until that problem was solved. The solution was to make the Executive responsible to the Assembly on matters of local interest so that it could only remain in office if it had the support of a majority of the members of the Assembly. On matters of imperial interest it would continue to be responsible to London.

When Howe read the Durham Report in March 1839 his own nascent ideas about responsible government crystallized, and he immediately became one of its greatest champions. On 16 October 1839 London sent somewhat vague instructions to the Governor of British North America, Charles Thompson, saying that the members of the Executive Council should not hold office simply because the governor had confidence in them. In Nova Scotia Lieutenant Governor Sir Colin Campbell refused to appoint an Executive Council that reflected the composition of the Assembly. The Reformers then passed a resolution calling for his recall, in effect launching a political rebellion against the Lieutenant Governor.

Campbell was replaced by Lucius Bentinck Falkland, a man whose lack of common sense quickly added to the increasingly confused situation. The Reformers had won the election of 1840 by 30 seats to the Tories 20, but Tories continued to hold all the positions in the Executive Council. Great Britain's next proposal was to have the governor appoint Councilors from both parties so that the Executive would represent the views of both factions. Lieutenant Governor Falkland duly appointed Howe and three other Reformers.

That experiment failed. The majority in the Executive was still Tory and the Reform majority in the Assembly would not pass its legislation. Many Reformers said that having token representation in the Executive did not create responsible government. When Falkland received conflicting advice from Tory and Reform Councilors, he accepted the former, and he appointed their friends alone to government jobs. In 1843 the experiment ended when Howe and the other Reformers resigned from the Executive.

The election of 1843 was won by Premier James Johnston and the Tories. Governor Falkland continued to make serious political blunders, and one of his key ministers, J.B Uniacke, resigned and joined the Reformers. In the 1846 Speech from the Throne Falkland made derogatory comments about two of the Reform leaders, another unacceptable interference in provincial politics. Howe apparently lost his temper and suggested that someone might be hired to beat up the Lieutenant Governor. Falkland had also misinformed London saying that the Reformers did not even have a leader. Howe immediately announced that J.B. Uniacke was their leader. That put the lie to Falkland's assertion, and he retired in disgrace.

In the meantime, Britain's views on the whole issue had changed. Until then Britain had managed the trade of the whole empire to its own advantage.

To do that it felt that it had to have complete control over colonial governments to prevent them from taking actions that might damage British economic interests. In the 1830s and 1840s Britain abolished that system of trade regulation, replacing it with free trade. It also began reducing its contribution to the defence of the colonies, and demanding that they assume a greater share of the burden. Both changes suggested that the colonies could and should have greater authority over for local affairs.

On 3 November 1846 the Colonial Secretary, Lord Earl Grey, told the new Governor, Sir John Harvey, that he was to ensure that any change to the Council reflected the wishes of people. Another election took place on 5 August 1847, a vicious, no-holds-barred campaign characterized by verbal abuse and physical violence. The main issue was responsible government. The Tories were so desperate that they hired a ship to distribute liquor along the eastern coast, and their candidate in Truro had 25 gallons of rum to win over the undecided. Howe led the Reformers to a clear majority of 29-22. In January 1848 the Governor asked the Reformers to form the government, and Nova Scotia became the first colony in the British Empire to have responsible government.

Other important steps were taken towards greater democracy. The franchise which had been limited to white men who owned property was gradually expanded by lowering the amount of property required. The practice of holding elections on successive days in different parts of each constituency had produced much violence and vote-buying. In the 1847 election all voting was held on the same day. Many rural constituencies elected Haligonians to represent them because it was too expensive to travel to Halifax for the Assembly sittings. That problem was solved when allowances were voted to cover the costs of being an MLA. With all those problems solved Nova Scotia set out on the bold experiment of governing itself on matters of local interest.

Chapter Five

Railroads, Schools, and Confederation, 1850-1867

Responsible government brought a revolutionary change in the way the administration operated. The governors accepted that power over local issues now rested in the hands of the party with majority support in the Assembly, namely the Reformers or Liberals. Joseph Howe was their undisputed leader, but he had had too many liabilities to be premier. James B. Uniacke therefore became premier. One of the new government's first acts was to reform the judiciary and remove incompetent judges. The government was reorganized, the number of office holders reduced, and their salaries significantly slashed.

The Reform MLAs wanted a wholesale purge of civil servants to open positions for their friends and supporters. Howe argued that only a few who were overly partisan should be removed. When the Conservatives returned to power in 1857 they dismissed some prominent Liberal appointees, and the Liberals returned the favour in 1860. Gradually it became the practice that a change in government resulted in a major change in office holders, a practice essential to the development of disciplined parties.

Uniacke was not a particularly inspiring leader, and Howe soon left the government. William Young became premier in April 1854 and led the Liberals to another victory in 1855 with 33 of the 53 seats. His ministry was then destroyed by religious issues. The school system consisted of private schools run by the different churches. Young introduced a proposal to establish a secular school system including Catholic separate schools. His Protestant ministers opposed the separate schools, and his two Catholic ministers resigned.

In another incident some Catholics beat up 20 members of a Presbyterian work crew who had been insulting them. The jury found them not-guilty, and the *Halifax Catholic* gloated that Protestants could no longer insult the Catholic religion. That provoked Howe to say that any Nova Scotian could say anything he wanted about any religion, and that further alienated Catholics from the Reform party. Then Young dismissed a Catholic civil servant, William Condon, for publicly supporting the Catholic rioters. Eight Catholic MLAs deserted the government and it was defeated in February 1857.

The government's defeat brought James Johnston back to the premier's office, but his government accomplished little. The following election, called for 12 May 1859, was fought almost exclusively on religion. The Catholics solidly supported Conservative candidates, but many Protestants deserted the

Conservatives. The Liberals won a thin majority of 29 out of 55 seats. Howe finally became premier, but his government achieved little and he soon left to become British Commissioner of Fisheries in Washington.

In the 1850s the 350,000 people of Nova Scotia were prosperous, contented and confident, enjoying a period often referred to as the province's Golden Age. Optimism stemmed in part from technological advances such as the telegraph, the increased use of steamships, better roads, and the new technological wonder, railways. Coal mining was developing into an important basis of the economy. A Reciprocity Treaty signed with the United States in 1854 allowed free access for agricultural products, timber, and fish, and exports of those commodities boomed. Then in the early 1860s the American Civil war created strong and sustained demand for Nova Scotia's exports.

The most important economic development of this period was railway construction. Geography and technology were not major problems but finding sufficient capital was. The market was not large enough to make railways profitable for private investors, and a mix of private and government-built lines gradually emerged. Both political parties discovered that the construction and operation of railways created enormous opportunities to reward party supporters with jobs and contracts, both of which then ensured a flow of money and support to the party at election time.

The first railway was built in 1839 to connect some coal mines with Pictou harbour. In the early 1850s the Liberal government began constructing a line from Halifax to Truro which was completed in 1858. A year later a line connected Halifax and Windsor. In the 1863 election the Conservatives promised to build lines from Truro to Pictou and from Windsor to Annapolis Royal. While these lines almost bankrupted the province, they were completed by 1868. A major challenge that preoccupied the province's politicians was connecting their railways to the rest of British North America via a line known as the Intercolonial Railway or ICR. Eventually the new federal government completed the ICR to Halifax as part of the Confederation deal.

The 1863 election was arguably the most important in the history of Nova Scotia and one of the most important in Canada. That election determined that Nova Scotia would join Confederation thereby ensuring its success. The Conservatives entered the fray under the de facto leadership of Charles Tupper. They were united, experienced, determined and well organized. The Liberals entered the race is disarray and without a leader. Just before the election Howe decided to run, but he was defeated. Tupper's Conservatives won 40 of 55 seats to 14 Liberals. With that massive majority he could begin implementing his promises of educational reform, railway construction, and union with other British North American provinces.

Tupper's immediate priority was education. In 1864 he passed the Free School Act establishing a single English-only non-denominational school system providing every child the right to primary education. The system came under the control of Cabinet which meant that Catholics could influence its managemen, and the Catholics accepted that system. That 1864 legislation provided provincial help to those municipalities that implemented the new policy. Few of them did, so one year later Tupper passed legislation forcing municipalities to raise taxes to match the provincial grants.

On 28 March 1864 Premier Tupper set Nova Scotia and Canada on the course that led to Confederation. He wrote the premiers of New Brunswick and PEI proposing a meeting to discuss the union of the Maritime provinces. The idea of a union of British North American colonies had been debated for decades, one question being whether it would be limited to the Maritimes or include Canada and Newfoundland. Tupper's preference was for the larger union, but tactically it was better to propose the smaller one first.

Tupper believed that small colonies were severely restricted both politically and economically. It would be better for them to unite in one big colony with a larger population, a single parliament, common laws, one postal service and currency, and no economic barriers to divide them. Such a colony would be able to finance the intercolonial railway, and that railway would unite the economies and peoples of the single large colony. Tupper never deviated from this vision, never questioned its wisdom, never weighed the advantages against some obvious disadvantages. Over the next three years he used other arguments as expedients but to him confederation was the right course, the inevitable course, and he would do everything he could to make it happen.

Few Maritimers shared his views. They liked their separate identities; their trade was with the wider world; and they had more in common with New England than with Canada. In Great Britain and in Canada, however, the idea of a confederation of all the colonies enjoyed strong support. Governor General Monck therefore wrote to Nova Scotia's Lieutenant Governor William MacDonnel asking if Canadian delegates could come to the Maritime meeting that Tupper had proposed. The three Maritime governments then decided to hold the meeting in Charlottetown and to invite the Canadians. Tupper selected the Nova Scotian delegation, including himself, the Liberal leaders of both the Assembly and the Legislative Council, the Conservative leader of the Legislative Council, and the Attorney General.

The meeting began on September 1, 1864. Canada sent a strong delegation fully prepared to advocate the larger scheme. On the first day Tupper presented his proposals for a union of the three Maritime colonies. Few were interested, and the Canadians then presented the case for a larger union. The delegates did not discuss details, but a great deal of time was spent on lavish entertainment, great quantities of alcohol were consumed, great speeches were made, and visions of a strong and growing colony stretching from sea to sea suddenly seemed within their grasp. They agreed to meet a month later in Quebec City to fill in the details, and all set off for a tour of Nova Scotia and New Brunswick.

At the Quebec City Conference the Canadian delegates had a relatively consistent view of the kind of a federation they wanted to create, and they had their way on almost all of the issues. It would be called the Dominion of Canada and would have a strong central government. Those provinces that joined would transfer to it responsibility for managing issues of overall importance such as the economy, intercolonial transportation, customs, currency, postal services, and criminal courts. The provinces would retain responsibility for local issues such as transportation, natural resources, commerce, economic development, education, family and property law, and local government.

The new federal House of Commons would be based on representation by population giving central Canada an overwhelming majority of Members of Parliament or MPs. Nova Scotia would have 19 of the 195 seats, but that proportion would decline as Canada expanded to the Pacific. Protecting the small Maritime populations in such a government became a major issue. The American model provided for a strong indirectly-elected Senate which could balance the power of the elected assembly. The Canadian delegates opposed this because it would weaken central Canada's influence. The Maritime delegates accepted that the Senate would be appointed by the central government. As such it provided a check on the House of Commons but did not really represent the provinces.

The main debate was over the number of Senators per province. The central Canadians wanted each region to have the same number of seats. They wanted the Maritimes to be treated as one region, with Upper and Lower Canada to be treated as separate regions. This was agreed, with Upper Canada (Ontario), Lower Canada (Quebec) and the Maritimes each obtaining 24 Senators, ten of the Maritime ones coming from Nova Scotia. That agreement meant that the Senate would not be able to protect the Maritime provinces. It is not clear why Maritime delegates agreed to something New Englanders would never have accepted in the American Constitution, namely, a near-complete loss of power.

Another major issue was the question of the subsidies the provinces would obtain from Ottawa in return for giving the federal government the sole right to collect customs. Customs provided 80% of Nova Scotia's income, and it would still have important and expensive activities to finance. On the basis of 1864 figures it was agreed that Ottawa would give all provinces an annual grant of 80 cents per capita.

This formula did not reflect the realities of either current colonial finances or the new division of responsibilities. Trade was far more important to the Maritime colonies than to Canada, so customs constituted a much larger proportion of revenue in the Maritimes. On the other hand, natural resources were far more important to Canada, so Ontario and Quebec retained more of their pre-Confederation revenue than did the Maritimes. The use of 1864 figures as a basis for calculations seriously distorted the formula because the American Civil War had produced a short-term export boom which benefitted the Maritimes more than Canada. The net effect was that a per capita grant of 80 cents to all provinces left the Maritime provinces with far less money than needed to maintain services at pre-confederation levels while it gave Ontario and Quebec far more money than they needed. That formula coupled with central Canada's overwhelming majorities in both House of Commons and Senate was a recipe for financial disaster for the Maritimes.

The Nova Scotian delegation seems to have been oblivious to the problems the Quebec Resolutions posed for the Maritimes. They did not fight hard to strengthen the Senate, to obtain equal representation, or to obtain a larger per capita grant. Nova Scotians leaned of the terms only when they were published in the newspapers on 19 November 1864. Opposition immediately developed among ordinary Nova Scotians in the fishing villages that traded across the Atlantic and saw little future in trade with Canada.

One of the Liberal politicians, William Annand, broke ranks with his party. He took control of two of the main Halifax newspapers, the *Chronicle* and the *Novascotian*, and reversed their editorial policy. He pointed out that the 80 cent subsidy represented only 25% of the customs revenue Nova Scotia would lose and would not even cover the existing roads budget. Annand argued that Canada would spend the customs revenue collected in Nova Scotia buying the Northwest Territories and building canals, and Nova Scotia's contingent of 19 MPs would not be able to influence federal policy.

This opposition developed into an organized political movement, well financed by the merchants. Their arguments began to take on coherence. Nova Scotia was a trading province and its markets were across the seas, not in Canada. It would be losing sovereignty over its own affairs to a parliament dominated by central Canadians. A united Canada would probably raise tariffs, raise costs and stunt the growth of Maritime industry. The anti-confederate campaign lacked leadership until Joseph Howe decided to fill that void. In January 1865 Howe began criticizing the arrangements in a series of letters published anonymously in the *Novascotian*. He did not, however, become the formal leader of the Antis until May, six months after opposition to Confederation first arose.

Tupper knew he would lose an election on the issue, but he did not have to call one until 1867. He did not submit the Quebec Resolutions to the Assembly, and Confederation was not even mentioned in the 1866 Speech from the Throne. When the inadequacies of the subsidy were raised, Tupper said he would fix that in the next round of negotiations.

The mystery in the entire process is why a majority of MLAs agreed to the most important change in Nova Scotia's history when that proposal was patently flawed and strongly opposed by the vast majority of the population. Tupper's colleagues on the delegation seem to have been influenced by the entertainment and camaraderie at the conferences and the sense that they were creating something wonderful. Some shared Tupper's belief that Nova Scotia would be better off as a small province in a large colony than as a separate colony. The threat of invasion by the United States when the Civil War ended was a factor in Britain's desire to see the colonies united, but Confederation was not needed to raise militias, build defences or transfer troops between colonies.

In 1865 some anti-English Irish insurgents known as Fenians launched attacks on Canada and New Brunswick from the United States, attacks which did not threaten Nova Scotia. Nevertheless, Governor Sir Fenwick Williams called out the militia which frightened some reluctant MLAs into believing that Confederation was necessary to defend the colony. Many of the MLAs, however, appear to have been bought off with offers of appointment as Senator or federal judge or of being elected as MPs. In spite of these inducements their acceptance of the terms remains a mystery because PEI and Newfoundland rejected Confederation and New Brunswick voted against it in an election. Confederation could not succeed without Nova Scotia which gave its delegates a powerful bargaining position. Its politicians simply failed to negotiate an acceptable deal.

In the meantime Tupper had put the province in a position where it was almost forced to accept Confederation. His very ambitious policies for education and railway construction increased the provincial debt by 50% in the two years before Confederation. The budget of 1866 indicated that expenditure would exceed revenue by $330,000, an enormous deficit for the time. Tupper

Chapter Four

Responsible Government, 1814-1850

The Treaty of Ghent which ended the War of 1812-14 did not lead to any significant changes of sovereignty, borders, or trading privileges in Nova Scotia. That meant, however, that the United States had failed for the second and final time to conquer the British North American colonies. After the war Britain reduced its wartime spending, but by the 1820s the Nova Scotian economy was growing once more. An important factor was a relaxation in British trade laws which had previously restricted Nova Scotian production, exports and shipping.

The traditional staples of fishing, agriculture, and forestry were doing well because production had increased, prices were good, and new markets were being developed. Ship building was becoming a major industry in almost every port, producing well-paid jobs and spin offs in lumbering, sail making, and carpentry. The ships were loaded with exports, sailed to their destination, and both ship and cargo sold leading to another cycle of shipbuilding and export. Nova Scotians finally began to compete seriously with Great Britain and New England in the Atlantic carrying trade.

One of the most successful of the new entrepreneurs was Samuel Cunard. Cunard's vision and daring made him a pioneer in steamboat innovation. In 1838 he won the contract to deliver mail between Britain and North America, and founded the Cunard Line, one of the greatest shipping companies in the world. Also reflecting the dynamism and openness of the day was the career of Alexander Keith. He founded a brewery on Water Street which is still a Halifax landmark, and rose up through society to become mayor of Halifax.

Other developments were diversifying the economy. In 1827 the General Mining Association opened a coal mine in Pictou and later developed more coal mines in the Sydney area. Coal mining soon became an important economic activity, feeding the increasing demand from steam ships, railways, and industry. Blacksmith shops were expanding into small industries producing simple implements for farm and home. Still worried about the American threat, the British Government decided to rebuild the Halifax Citadel in stone, an undertaking that stimulated the economy for three decades.

In 1826 the dream of creating an economic hinterland for the Halifax region began to take shape when construction started on the Shubenacadie

Canal. The construction contributed to economic growth and a sense of confidence and optimism. The eastern terminus was Dartmouth which developed into an industrial hub. In 1830 the first steamboat built in British North America was launched in Dartmouth, inaugurating a ferry service to Halifax. Roads to Truro, Windsor and eventually Yarmouth and Sydney reduced travel time and costs. The economic growth led to the founding of the Halifax Banking Company in 1825 and the Bank of Nova Scotia in 1832.

In the early nineteenth century three new waves of immigration changed the demographic makeup of the colony, and swelled the population to 125,000 by 1830 and 270,000 by 1848. During the war of 1812 Britain offered freedom to American slaves, and 2,000 of them joined the existing Black community. Highland Scots continued to settle in eastern Nova Scotia. Even more immigrants came from Catholic Ireland, most settling in Halifax where they became the city's working class. Their lives centered on the church and a range of religious institutions providing for all aspects of life – social, educational, cultural, and philanthropic. Like the Acadians, New Englanders and Scots before them, they came to make a better life and they did so, steadily bettering themselves and their children.

This period of immigration came to an end in 1840, and Nova Scotia's demographic pattern has changed little since then. The largest group was Scottish, both Highland Catholic concentrated in the east and Lowland Presbyterians west of Pictou and in the central region, some 30% of the province's present-day population. The second largest ethnic group was English, Loyalists who were primarily Anglican, New-England Planters, plus a steady trickle of immigrants from England, their descendents now constituting 28% of today's population.

Next were the Irish, concentrated in Halifax, one-fifth of today's Nova Scotians. The Acadians survived, concentrated around Yarmouth and in isolated communities such as Arichat and Cheticamp in Cape Breton, accounting for 16% of the province's population. The most visible ethnic minority was African Nova Scotians concentrated in Africville and other communities in the Halifax area. The Mi'kmaq were pushed farther and farther into the most inferior areas of the interior and decimated by poverty, disease, neglect, and discrimination. In spite of this, they maintained their identity and eventually began expanding, now representing 3% of the population.

The province's religious character was also determined by 1840. The Protestant majority was divided into a number of denominations so Roman Catholicism is the largest single religious sect, accounting for 37% of today's refused to release the figures because the only way that debt could be handled was if the new federal government took responsibility for it.

Another key factor in Nova Scotia's acquiescence was that Britain was determined to force the colonies to unite. Lieutenant Governor MacDonnell was ordered to support Confederation but refused because doing so meant siding with one party in a domestic debate. He was removed and his successor, Sir Fenwick Williams, understood that his job was to promote Confederation. He interfered with the anti-confederate campaign, and supported Tupper with lavish entertainment and strong hints of appointments for MLAs who favoured the scheme. A number of MLAs were seen at Government House, changed sides on the issue, and later received rewards such as Senate appointments.

Tupper could not, however, prevent any debate in the Assembly. He therefore introduced a motion in April 1866, cleverly calling for Maritime union rather than Confederation. William Miller, an independent MLA who had opposed Confederation, suddenly introduced a motion calling for the appointment of a delegation to attend the final round of negotiations in London where it could seek better terms. If the Assembly approved the delegation, it would in fact be approving Confederation. The crucial vote carried 31 to 19. The majority of 31 included six Conservatives and one independent who had previously opposed Confederation. Without their change of heart the motion would have been defeated 26 to 24. It is still not clear why Miller and the others changed sides, but the strong suspicion is that they were bought off.

At the subsequent negotiations in London in late 1866, Tupper failed to obtain any significant improvements to the terms. Howe and other opponents of Confederation spent months lobbying British politicians and the media with no success. Those negotiations actually weakened the Maritime provinces even more as fisheries was made an exclusive federal responsibility rather than a shared one such as agriculture. Given the importance of fisheries to the Maritime economies, that left them weaker than the provinces where agriculture was a more important economic function. On July 1 1867, Nova Scotian politicians took their province into a disastrous arrangement, moved to Ottawa to enjoy the fruits of their labours, and left others to deal with the aftermath.

Chapter Six
Anti-Confederation, 1867-1882

Confederation came into effect on 1 July 1867. The status Nova Scotia had enjoyed for 150 years as a separate British colony was over, and now it was merely one of four provinces in the larger colony of Canada. Some observers have equated Confederation with independence or the creation of a new nation. In fact, Canada would not become independent until Great Britain passed the Statute of Westminster in 1931. When Canadians became a nation is debatable, but for many decades Nova Scotians attached higher priority to their provincial identity than to membership in a new nation of Canadians. On 1 July 1867 Confederation was generally met with anger or indifference. Tupper and other politicians were burnt in effigy, editorials moaned the death of a proud colony, and gloomy predictions were made about the future. For decades Nova Scotia refused to make July 1st a school holiday.

By mid-1867 Tupper's government had made many of the administrative changes required by the British North America Act. The size of the assembly was reduced from 55 to 38 members, the size of the cabinet from five to four. The major courts became federal ones. On July 4 Tupper was replaced by a new premier, Hiram Blanchard, but Tupper postponed the provincial election until the federal elections had been held in Ontario, Quebec and New Brunswick. The federal Conservatives under John A. Macdonald won a strong majority in those elections. That meant that when Nova Scotians went to the polls on 18 September to elect both federal MPs and provincial MLAs, Confederation was a fait accompli.

The coalition that opposed Confederation decided to contest all 38 provincial and 19 federal seats. Their leaders were Joseph Howe at the federal level and William Annnad in the the provincial wing. Their only goal was to convince Britain to allow Nova Scotia to withdraw from the arrangement. The Confederates or Unionists entered the 1867 election saddled with the blame for the terms and for the way they had been forced on the province. They were accused of bribing their opponents, lying to London, and abusing the lieutenant governor's powers. The results took even the Antis by surprise. Federally the Confederates won only Tupper's seat. The other 18 new MPs were determined to take the province out of Confederation. Provincially the Antis won 36 of the 38 seats.

The Anti MPs and MLAs met to review their phenomenal success and to decide on a strategy. The new MPs decided to go to Ottawa so they could represent the province in Parliament even though that meant accepting

Confederation in principle. The provincial MLAs decided to form a provincial government, William Annand becoming premier on 7 November. They decided to send a delegation to London under Howe and Annand to convince the British government that Nova Scotia had been forced into Confederation against its will. Howe and Annand met politicians, journalists and other influential people, but they discovered that Britain was completely committed to Confederation and had no intention of seeing it unravel.

Ottawa sent Tupper to convince Howe to change sides and accept that the best he could do was obtain some improvements or "better terms". Howe would then gain the credit and a cabinet position in Ottawa. Other Anti MPs who accepted Confederation would be able to make many of the new federal patronage appointments of senators, judges, officials, and employees for the post office, customs and other departments and agencies. Gradually Howe and some other MPs accepted the political reality and the personal rewards.

The job of wooing Nova Scotia was rendered far more difficult by the way in which the new federal government implemented its mandate. Nova Scotia's tariff had been 10% compared to the old Canadian one of 15%. Ottawa applied the old Canadian rate, imposed it on more items and added taxes that were new to Nova Scotia, effectively raising the tax rate by over 50% with all the money flowing to Ottawa. Ottawa took over the Intercolonial Railway, and then raised the fares. The former Canada had applied the death penalty to more crimes than did Nova Scotia; Ottawa now applied those laws to all provinces. The few civil servants who retired from the old Canadian bureaucracy received pensions; the many who retired from the Nova Scotian administration did not. With one tenth of the new Canada's population Nova Scotians obtained only two of the 500 jobs in the new federal administration.

Nova Scotia's most serious grievance concerned the financial situation. After cutting the roads budget from $240,000 to $100,000 the province still had a deficit of $100,000. In contrast, Ontario had a surplus of $1,000,000 one year after Confederation. Indeed, by 1874 the province was spending over twice the amount Tupper had estimated it would need. Even the federal auditor said the figures accepted at the Quebec Conference were woefully inadequate

In 1868 Ottawa and Howe began to discuss "better terms". Ottawa offered an additional $82,968 per year, the same amount New Brunswick had obtained in 1866. Howe accepted the offer in December 1868. It did not come close to closing the gap, and it would only last a decade while the provincial surrender of customs revenue would last forever. Macdonald negotiated the deal with Howe and refused to deal with any provincial politician to make the point that MPs rather than provincial governments represented the provinces in

Ottawa. Macdonald visited Halifax to meet Howe, but refused to meet Premier Annand. It was clear that Howe would enter the federal cabinet, so "better terms" were agreed between the Prime Minister and his new minister-in-waiting. Annand's government had no choice but to swallow its pride and accept the deal.

One by one the federal MPs were bought off with positions or influence, increasingly estranged from their provincial counterparts. Howe was appointed to the federal cabinet, an appointment that had to be approved by his constituency through a by-election. Howe was seen as a traitor by the Antis, and the campaign was extremely bitter, nasty and personal. Ottawa spent an estimated $30,000 in bribes and the Antis spent $20,000, enormous sums amounting to around $25.00 per vote cast, equal to over half the annual "better terms" Howe had obtained for the entire province. Howe narrowly won re-election, but the effort broke his health.

Escaping from Confederation was the only goal of the new provincial government. Now it had to get on with the business of administering its limited responsibilities. The best and most experienced politicians had left for Ottawa. Premier Annand was a weak leader, somewhat short of genuine principles, and subject to frequent accusations of shady business dealing. In four years in office this motley assortment of politicians achieved very little. One exception was the adoption of secret balloting in 1870, introduced to prevent the federal government from rigging elections.

The 1871 election saw some political realignment. The Antis, now known as the Nova Scotia Party, were in fact the old Liberal Party. The Anti's public support fell from 58.6% to 52.2% and they lost 12 seats for a total of 24. Five of those losses were extremists who preferred annexation to the United States to provincial status within Canada. The Conservatives became an effective party once more, gaining 12 seats for a total of 14 based on an increase of only 5% in popular support.

Annand's government then concentrated on constructing railway lines. He supported the federal Liberals in the 1874 election and expected support from them when they replaced John A. Macdonald's Conservative government. On that assumption Annand called a snap election for December 1874 promising to build a line from New Glasgow to the Strait of Canso. He gained a little in public support but lost one seat, defeating the Conservatives by 24 to 14 seats. The federal government then announced that it preferred to build a railway on Cape Breton Island leaving Annand's railway policy in ruins.

In late 1874 Annand sought to strengthen his lackluster government by recruiting a Conservative, Phillip Carteret Hill. He was a rich, cultivated, well-educated gentleman whose pride and modest sense of civic duty outweighed his mediocre political skills. Hill became premier when Annand retired on 11 May 1875. Hill's biggest problem was the straightjacket imposed on the province by the totally inadequate federal subsidy. He also took over at the beginning of an economic slowdown which turned into a full recession by 1877. Hill repeatedly begged the new Liberal government in Ottawa for more money, but Ottawa showed no sympathy. The "better terms" of $82,968 annually came to an end on 1 July 1877. When Hill asked for an extension Ottawa refused saying that governments had to live by the agreements they signed.

The province desperately needed extensions to several railways to fill in the gaps in the overall network. Three were proposed or under construction: the Eastern Extension running from New Glasgow to the Strait of Canso, an extension of the Western Counties Railway running southwest from Annapolis to Yarmouth, and a line from Middletown in the Annapolis Valley to Bridgewater on the Atlantic called the Nova Scotia Central Railway or NSCR. The federal government had established a special fund to support such railways, but it was almost exhausted. Ottawa finally completed the Intercolonial in 1876, and it clearly felt it had done enough in terms of supporting railways.

The loss of both the federal railway fund and "better terms" reduced the provincial budget by $180,000. Without further federal support work stopped on two of the railways and wages were not paid on the third. This financial mess provided the Conservatives with ample ammunition for a relentless attack on the government. At the end of the four-year term Hill called an election for 17 September 1878. His party lost 16 of their 24 seats based on a decline in popular support from 54% to 45%. Conservatives support jumped from 43 to 52%, their seat total rising from 14 to 30.

The new provincial premier, Simon Hugh Holmes, was a poor manager of men, lacked charisma and political judgment, and acted without consultation. The situation he inherited was worse than that of his three predecessors because Hill had spent the entirety of the 1878 budget plus $156,000 from the 1879 budget. Before leaving office, Hill filled all the vacancies in the Legislative Council with Liberals who blocked some of the legislation that Holmes introduced. Holmes thought that the new Conservative government in Ottawa would be more sympathetic, but it treated him as though he were a political enemy. Holmes wrote the federal government to explain the financial situation and ask for help with railway construction. There was no reply.

The province found money to complete the extension from Digby to Yarmouth but it was not yet connected to other lines. Thirty miles of the Eastern Extension from New Glasgow had been completed but it was not functioning properly because of disputes with the federal government over connections with the Intercolonial Railway. Holmes then addressed another major problem with the railways. All the lines had been built on an ad hoc basis with no master plan. Some were private and some were public, some were provincially-owned and some were federal, and they lacked proper connections between them. Holmes decided that the province should take over all the pieces and create a single trunk line from Yarmouth to Sydney with the other sections as branch lines. That network would then be sold to a private company which would solve both the railway problem and the financial crisis. Unfortunately the complex set of negotiations failed.

Faced with federal intransigence on subsidies Holmes cut spending by a further 40% and finally balanced the budget. Paradoxically that success undermined the argument that the province needed larger subsidies. Holmes also tackled a basic flaw in the overall administration of the province, namely the weakness of municipal government and their reliance on the provincial government to build local infrastructure. He forced the municipalities to levy direct taxes to pay for local roads. That transferred $55,000 in spending from the provincial to local governments, and made the latter directly responsible to their own electors for spending and taxation. It was a necessary but deeply unpopular move, and it transferred patronage from Conservative MLAs to the municipalities which tended to be staffed with Liberals.

The Conservative government was less successful with another piece of unfinished business. Hill had tried to resolve the problem of government support for higher education by building a non-denominational University of Halifax. Holmes dropped that idea and introduced legislation designed to bring some common standards to higher education. The Anglicans objected to any inspection of King's College; the Presbyterians thought Dalhousie's grant was too large; some Protestants objected to any grants to Catholic colleges; and some still wanted a single university. Holmes could not obtain any consensus and the government stopped funding colleges altogether.

Holmes had made too many mistakes and on 23 May 1882 his own backbenchers replaced him with John Thompson. Thompson called an election for 20 June 1882, the same day as the federal one, hoping that the popularity of Sir John A. Macdonald's federal Conservatives would carry the provincial party to victory. The federal Conservatives did indeed win 14 of 21 seats but Thompson went down to defeat winning only 14 seats to the Liberal's 24. Thomson resigned after just 54 days as premier but later became Prime Minister of Canada.

Chapter Seven

Liberal Forever, 1882-1914

The election of a Conservative government in 1878 was an anomaly, and in 1882 the electorate turned back to the Liberals even though they had no leader, no program and no solutions to the province's problems. Only nine of the 24 Liberal MLAs had experience, but the caucus selected one of the new members as premier, 32-year-old William Pipes. Oddly this rather pathetic beginning evolved into the most successful political regime in Canadian history, winning ten successive elections. Pipes was soon replaced by William Fielding who ran the province effortlessly from 1884 to 1896, and then by George Murray who ran it effortlessly from 1896 until 1923, setting a record for longevity in any British parliamentary system that still stands.

Pipes immediately tackled the intractable railways problem. He borrowed several million dollars to buy the Pictou branch from the federal government and to complete the Eastern Extension from Pictou to the Strait of Canso. This plan failed and Pipes sold the Eastern Extension to the federal government. He then turned to the equally intractable problem of the inadequate subsidies. The province made a detailed study of the situation and sent it to Ottawa. Pipes and Fielding travelled to Ottawa and wrote long letters to federal cabinet ministers. The response was negative. Unable to solve problems or manage his fractious party, Pipes resigned on 14 July 1884, recommending that Fielding be his successor. Fielding had certain qualities that his five predecessors lacked, namely strength of personality, tact, honesty, flexibility, determination, common sense and political savvy. These skills made him premier for 12 years, a dominant federal politician for a further two decades, and almost made him Prime Minister of Canada.

Fielding's strategy for forcing Ottawa to provide larger subsidies was to threaten secession. He warned Ottawa that if better terms were not forthcoming he would make secession the main issue in the upcoming election. Ottawa ignored him, and he called the election winning an overwhelming victory and increasing his seat total from 24 to 29 and his popular vote from 52% to 55%. Fielding's provincial electoral triumph was followed by a federal election in February 1887 in which the Nova Scotias Conservatives won 14 of 21 seats, seriously undermining the province's case. It is not clear what difference a Liberal sweep of the federal seats would have made. There would have been more petitions and visits to London where the imperial government would certainly have rejected once again the idea of undoing Confederation. Fielding's secession movement seemed to be more about burying the issue and solidifying his own political positions and that of his party than actually taking the province out of Canada. As such, it was a resounding success.

Fielding then turned to solving the province's financial problem through initiatives that lay within provincial control. Though coal was found in abundance in near Sydney, Springhill and New Glasgow, it had not been developed. In the late nineteenth century demand began to increase because of railways, steamships, and industrialization. Fielding increased the royalty on coal from 7 to 10 cents per ton, producing an immediate jump in provincial revenues. A Boston entrepreneur, Henry Whitney, became interested in Cape Breton coal and his Dominion Coal Company obtained a 99-year lease on all mines on the island. In return, the Nova Scotia government received a 12 cent royalty per ton. Whitney began investing substantially, and coal production rose from 700,000 tons in 1875 to 1,700,000 tons in 1890 and 3,000,000 tons by 1902. Royalties from coal rose from $487,000 in 1903 to $619,000 in 1904 finally passing the value of federal subsidies.

The coal industry was also assisted by Canadian tariffs which gave it preferred access to the eastern Quebec market, and by preferential rates on the Intercolonial Railway. Later the markets in both New England and Quebec declined and the company created new ones by investing in transportation and gas systems in Halifax and a new steel industry in Cape Breton. The latter, the Dominion Iron and Steel Company, became one of the largest companies in Canada.

The combination of railway construction, the industrial revolution, the federal National Policy, and easy access to cheap coal began to produce an economic boom along the Eastern Extension Railway. Major steel industries developed in Sydney and Pictou. Amherst became a centre for the manufacture of railway cars for the whole of Canada, and New Glasgow was a booming industrial city with three factories making glass and a plethora of other industries. While the population of Nova Scotia barely increased in the 1880s, these cities grew by over 50%.

Fielding was sympathetic to the conditions of workers, and became friends with Robert Drummond, Secretary General of the Provincial Workmen's Association. Fielding introduced progressive labour legislation which provided a minimum age for child labour, a maximum 60-hour work week, pay day every two weeks, minimum safety regulations, and compulsory arbitration. The safety regulations were extremely important because in the 1870s one miner in 40 was killed in mining accidents. These improvements did not, however, solve the main problems in the mining industry, and disasters and strikes would continue to characterize the industry throughout its history.

The increased revenue gave the province something it had not had since before Confederation, namely significant sums to invest in railroads. With the additional revenue from coal royalties, Fielding was able to tackle the problems of the remaining railway branch lines. The West Counties Railway from Annapolis to Digby was finally finished and incorporated into the rest of the network. The line from Middleton in the Annapolis Valley to Bridgewater on the Atlantic was completed in 1894. In 1890 the Eastern Extension, now part of the Intercolonial Railway, finally reached North Sydney where it connected to a ferry to Newfoundland. Plans were also launched for building the last link in the provincial network, namely a railway running south from Halifax. Known as the Halifax and Southwestern or HSW, it ran into the usual problems of delays, cost overruns, poor construction, and political interference, and was known to some as the Hellish Slow and Wobbly.

In the 1896 federal election Fielding campaigned strongly for the Liberals. They won, and Prime Minister Sir Wilfrid Laurier appointed Fielding as Finance Minister. Fielding proposed George Henry Murray to succeed him and the caucus reluctantly agreed. Murray was seen as an odd choice. He had failed four times to win a federal seat but the odds in each case were overwhelming. He was an excellent businessman, worked well with people, was conciliatory, moderate, and well-respected. He was not well known but he became an immensely successful premier, winning elections in 1897, 1901, 1906, 1911, 1916, and 1920. In 1923 he retired and burnt all his personal papers ensuring that little would ever be know about him other than his few notable political achievements, the chief of which was staying in power.

A number of factors explain why Nova Scotia became a one-party Liberal fiefdom. As the architects of Confederation, the Conservatives were punished for decades by the voters. Conservative domination of the federal government meant that good and ambitious Conservative politicians were attracted to Ottawa. Prime Minister Macdonald's high-handed treatment of Nova Scotia put the provincial Conservatives in the impossible position of defending unpopular federal policies, and Fielding mastered the art of campaigning provincially against the federal government. Provincial Liberal regimes provided solid, careful, responsible administration, slowly responding to public pressure on various issues, avoiding major scandals and evading issues that could seriously hurt them politically. Luck was a huge factor as both Fielding and Murray turned out to be superb politicians.

Another factor in the long Liberal reign was the advantage a governing party enjoys under the British parliamentary system. The Liberals had control of patronage which they used effectively. Before elections much of the roads budget could be spent in marginal constituencies. Old politicians could be rewarded with lucrative positions clearing the way for younger ones to renew the party. A plurality in any constituency secured that candidate's election, and the government arranged constituency borders to concentrate votes where they mattered. In fact, in the ten provincial elections between 1882 and 1925 the Liberals won over twice as many seats as did the Conservatives usually with less than 10% more of the popular vote. Sitting governments could call elections when circumstances were favourable. Since 1867 only seven of 29 elections led to a change of government, and in two of these the government was old and feeble and in two others it was in power during a depression.

Ideology did not, however, play a role in Liberal ascendency. There was little difference between the parties. Basically, they were the Ins and the Outs, and except in periods of recession people preferred to re-elect the Ins rather than take a chance on the inexperienced Outs. On many issues the Conservatives were more progressive or "liberal" than the Liberals. For decades the Conservatives fought for democratic issues such as universal adult male suffrage, woman's suffrage, electoral reform and the abolition of the unelected Legislative Council.

One issue that challenged both Fielding and Murray was prohibition. The excessive consumption of alcohol or "demon rum" was one of the most serious social problems in the nineteenth century. It was a major cause of death, accidents, loss of jobs, crime, violence, marriage break-up, poverty, disease and profound sadness. Liquor was consumed by the vast majority of the adult male population because of culture and habit, to ease pain, and to celebrate good times or drown sorrows. In the late nineteenth century a movement arose to perfect mankind, and one of its chief goals was to end the consumption of liquor. It was led by the evangelical Protestant denominations, the Baptists, Methodists, and Presbyterians and spearheaded by the Woman's Temperance Union. They demanded that government impose their moral values on members of their own congregations and indeed on the whole of the community.

In 1878 the federal government passed the Canadian Temperance or Scott Act prohibiting the sale of liquor in those municipalities that chose to adopt it. Within a decade the prohibition movement had forced most Nova Scotian counties to go "dry". Liquor consumption declined but many people simply went to a "wet" county, bought the liquor and took it home. Pressure mounted for the provincial government to tighten the loopholes, but Fielding and Murray avoided the pressure as best they could. Murray was finally forced to pass undemocratic legislation that required a two-thirds majority in a referendum in order for a county to approve a liquor licence for a tavern but only a one-quarter minority to cancel an existing licence.

By the early twentieth century 16 of 18 counties had gone dry, the main exception being Halifax where the large Catholic population did not share Protestant views about alcohol. In 1910 the provincial government announced that none of the licences outside Halifax would be renewed and that the number of licences for taverns in Halifax would be reduced from 90 to 70. Gradually the government was forced to tighten the rules until by 1918 it was illegal to buy alcohol throughout the province.

During the Fielding-Murray period urban and small-town Nova Scotia took on its present the appearance. Towns have a main street wide enough for four lanes of traffic, lined with two or three story stores. Important establishments such as banks were made of stone, less important ones of brick or wood. Towards the end of "downtown" are the churches, each with quite distinctive styles of architecture. There would be elementary and secondary schools, a high school and a public library, lodges for the Protestant Orange Order, the Catholic Knights of Columbus, or the Masons, and a town hall for civic functions. The residential sections would contain three story houses for the rich, two storey houses for the middle class, and poor-quality homes for the working class. The arrival of railways required a station, warehouse and coal and lumber yards, and the development of small industry created another new section in the town. Town life was made complete with a park, a rink for skating, hockey and curling, fairgrounds, and a track for horse racing.

In the early twentieth century these towns acquired much of the modern infrastructure that still serves them. Gradually streets and sidewalks were paved and illuminated with gas and later electric lights. Sewers and water mains brought dramatic improvements to public health. Electricity and telephones arrived before World War I. In Halifax tram lines allowed people to live farther and farther from the place of work, and were the mainstay of public transportation until after World War II when they were replaced by buses. Improved police, fire and hospital services gradually made life safer and healthier. After World War I cinemas and the radio came to supplement theatres and live music, and cars and trucks began to replace carriages and wagons.

During this period the economy of Nova Scotia gradually modernized. The mainstay in the golden age was global commerce based on shipping and the construction of wooden sailing ships. In the 1870s some 3,000 Nova Scotian vessels sailed the high seas, an astounding ratio of one ship for every 150 people. Though gradually replaced by iron-hulled steam ships, sailing ships remained competitive for cargo and the fishing industry until after World War II. The famous *Bluenose* built in the 1920s was one of the last of the great wooden schooners, famous for winning a series of races against American schooners.

Agriculture remained a main employer. Crops were diversified with the development of potatoes and apples as major exports. Most farmers had to supplement their income with seasonal fishing and work in the forests, though fishing and forestry were declining sectors of the economy. Manufacturing gradually developed particularly in textiles, where mills contributed to the incomes of a dozen towns all over the province. Like fishing and forestry, however, textiles did not produce many well-paying jobs. Heavy industry developed from Amherst to Sydney but was precarious because of distance from major markets and weaknesses in management.

This slow economic growth was not sufficient to absorb the natural increase in population, and after Confederation tens of thousands of Nova Scotians left the province. In the 1880s and 1890s the population grew by only 10,000. Significantly, most of the emigration consisted of skilled workers and young men and women leaving behind a disproportionate number of children and seniors. Nova Scotia entered a vicious circle from which it has never escaped, with a shrinking base of taxpayers supporting a growing number of consumers of government services. The inevitable result was that per capita government spending on services and infrastructure was inferior to that elsewhere prompting even more of the young and educated to emigrate. Rural depopulation was especially serious as marginal farms were abandoned and machinery replaced labour.

Halifax reflected the paradox of the province's economy. It never became the eastern terminus of Canada's transnational railway system because trade also passed through Saint John and Portland, Maine. It did not develop into a major commercial and manufacturing city because it did not service a large enough population. Its industry was concentrated in refining, distilling and brewing, on services and transportation, and on government. Halifax was the centre of Maritime financial institutions but these were gradually consolidated and their headquarters moved to central Canada, the Bank of Nova Scotia itself moving to Toronto in 1900. In 1906 the last British troops left the city bringing to and end British military spending which had been a mainstay of the economy since 1749. These underlying problems were, however, masked by modest population growth, construction and the arrival of modern amenities.

Prosperity returned in the 15 years before World War I when the province benefited from a prolonged global economic boom. Nova Scotia's population reached 460,000 in 1901 and 490,000 in 1911. Rapidly increasing royalties from coal, favourable adjustments to federal subsidies and new taxes gave the Murray government money to spend within a balanced budget. The completion of the railway network meant that the revenue could be spent on services. Schools, hospitals and libraries sprouted, including specialized institutions for the blind, deaf, aged and orphans and for tuberculosis. Higher education was broadened with the completion of the Agricultural College at Truro in 1905 and the Nova Scotia Technological College in 1909. That boom came to an end before the outbreak of World War I, and that war marked the beginning of two decades of economic decline.

Chapter Eight

War and Depression, 1914-1933

The outbreak of World War I on 4 August 1914 was welcomed in Nova Scotia. The province still saw itself as a very loyal member of the British Empire and had a long and valued tradition of military and naval service. Britain was now at war with a formidable opponent, Germany, and would need all the help it could get. Thousands of men immediately volunteered, and the wartime effort dominated every aspect of life in Nova Scotia for the next four years.

The departure of so many men changed society. It emptied high schools and university classes, took away husbands and fathers, and weakened the work force at a time when demand for all products was growing. To fill the gaps in the work force retired people went back to work while young boys and girls worked longer hours. Women began to take jobs never thought appropriate for the fairer sex, a change that eventually became permanent.

The war dominated politics. There was less time for petty squabbling and the government's legislative agenda was sparse. Much of what was done centered on supporting the war effort or reacting to wartime demands. For at least half a century women had been demanding the vote. Now it seemed hard to deny them. But the Murray government was dead-set against woman's suffrage, and women would have to wait until 1920 before they could have a say in elections. The poorest of men had also been excluded but in 1920 they too voted for the first time. The war also led to the final victory of the prohibitionists as selling liquor became illegal across the province.

As in every war since 1749 Halifax boomed as supplies from all over North America were dispatched for Britain and France. To counter the effectiveness of German submarines, convoys of ships were organized in Halifax harbor for the trans-Atlantic voyage, and the city filled with merchantmen and soldiers waiting for their ships to depart. All over the province ports and industrial towns became hives of activity, producing ships, ammunition, artillery and other forms of war material. Patriotism and support for the war swept the province and people joined volunteer organizations to help the war effort. Labour strife disappeared and so many coal miners volunteered to fight that the federal government had to stop recruiting them to maintain adequate coal production.

By 1917, however, that wartime enthusiasm had been undermined by seemingly endless sacrifice, by the unfairness of government policies, by inflation, and especially by the conscription crisis. During the war eight million

Canadians produced an army of over 500,000 which sustained over 60,000 killed. The danger of losing the war was very real and the Canadian Government decided to impose conscription to maintain its strength on the western front. Many in Nova Scotia agreed but others did not. Farmers were under tremendous pressure to produce more, and sought exemption for themselves and their sons. Throughout the province there was growing bitterness at the way ordinary people were being asked to sacrifice while the rich reaped windfall profits from wartime demand. The cost of living rose faster than incomes. More and more workers went on strike just to maintain their standard of living. In fact, the Maritimes were more hostile to conscription than any region other than Quebec.

Nova Scotia was the site of the greatest Canadian tragedy of the war. At 8.50 am on 6 December 1917 two ships collided in the harbour. One, the *Mont Blanc*, was packed with 2,000 tons of high explosives. It erupted in the largest man-made explosion prior to World War II. The explosion flattened 130 hectares of north-end Halifax destroying the main industrial area of the city, six thousand homes, and throwing material and people hundreds of meters. Almost 2,000 people were killed and another 7,000 wounded, as many casualties as Nova Scotia suffered in the war overseas. A massive rescue operation began with volunteers coming from hundreds of miles. So many people suffered eye injuries from flying glass that the medical knowledge leapt forward because of the intense experience of treating so many patients.

For years the war had been advertised as a struggle for democracy, the "war to end all wars", a tragedy whose sacrifice would be justified by the new and wonderful world that would be born of the ashes. By 1918 Nova Scotians were very skeptical of the promises, and their skepticism soon turned to anger and dismay. Victory celebrations were muted. Veterans were shocked by the sight of the devastation in Halifax, enraged by the late delivery of their back pay, and discouraged to find no jobs waiting for them. Women who had entered the workforce were dismissed to make way for the veterans, but staff cutbacks due to falling demand still left many veterans unemployed. There were riots in Halifax in March 1918, and more riots in February 1919 when soldiers and civilians destroyed restaurants and stores. These demonstrations merged into an unprecedented series of strikes in 1919-20, the one at Halifax Shipyards being one of the biggest in Canadian history.

Nova Scotia was in serious economic and social trouble, suffering high unemployment, falling prices for farm, forestry and fish products and rising labour unrest. But while the rest of Canada emerged from that postwar crisis to enjoy relative prosperity in the 1920s, Nova Scotia deteriorated into a genuine depression. From 1918 to 1921 employment in the Halifax shipyards fell from 2000 to 100, employment in manufacturing fell 42%, wooden shipbuilding declined 75%, fishermen lost their access to the American market, and BC lumber replaced local forestry products. In the 1920s the population of Nova Scotia stagnated at around 600,000.

The two worst affected sectors of the economy were coal mining and farming. Farmers were harmed by high prices for their inputs, falling prices for their crops, and the loss of their sons and daughters through migration to cities or outside the province. Rural depopulation was a major problem with fewer and fewer people available to sustain communities and local services. The farmers organized themselves into a political movement, the United Farmers of Nova Scotia, and decided to enter politics directly. By 1919 the problems in the coal mines were decades old with no solutions in sight. The market for coal was falling rapidly because of rising production costs and declining tariff protection. Labour decided to launch a political party in time for the next election.

Premier Murray had been in power since 1896 and was a masterful politician, his specialty being avoiding politically difficult problems. All over the province farmers were organizing for the election as was labour in the coal mining districts, and they agreed not to run candidates against each other. Murray called a snap election in 1920, and the Liberals managed to cling to power with 29 seats after seeing their popular vote drop from 50% to 44%. The farmers elected seven of their 16 candidates and Labour elected four of their 12. The Conservative vote fell from 48% to 23% and they won only three seats, so the Farmer-Labour group formed the official opposition.

The Farmer-Labour coalition was a dismal failure. The interests of the two groups were often opposed, with labour wanting high wages while farmers wanted lower costs. Farmers who worked over 12 hours a day had little sympathy for coal miners who demanded an eight-hour day. As the depression hit, unemployment decimated the ranks of the labour organizations and migration continued to weaken farming communities. The Farmer-Labour coalition proved incapable of forcing change and it quickly became almost irrelevant.

The most serious problem the government faced was in the Sydney area where labour unrest produced 58 strikes between 1920 and 1925. In 1920 the Cape Breton coal and steel companies were consolidated into the British Empire Steel Corporation (BESCO), for a time the largest industrial conglomerate in the British Empire. The local miners had recently won both recognition and pay raises, and breaking their union was a key goal of the new BESCO president Roy Wolvin. In 1921 he set out to force the workers to take a 37% pay cut. This produced riots throughout industrial Cape Breton, demonstrations at Provincial House in Halifax, and the emergence of very radical union leaders like J.B. MacLachlan.

The Liberal government dropped all pretence of neutrality and sided with management. In July 1922 the steelworkers went on strike to obtain recognition of their union. The government called in 600 troops to protect BESCO property and control the unrest. When the police attacked the workers, MacLachlan called out his 6,000 coal miners in sympathy. The American-based United Mine Workers headquarters did not advocate sympathy strikes and revoked the charter of the Sydney branch of the union. Some intemperate comments led to a charge of sedition, and MacLachlan was sentenced to two years in jail.

The failure of government to effectively address the region's economic problems produced the Maritime Rights Movement which dominated the politics of all three provinces in the 1920s. It highlighted traditional grievances like the tariffs that protected central Canadian industries while tariffs protecting Maritime products had declined so much that they were no longer competitive in central Canada. Federal subsidies which had always been inadequate were still falling, from 66% of provincial revenue in 1900 to only 11% by 1920. Another traditional grievance was that the federal government had never made Halifax the Atlantic equivalent of Vancouver, allowing the railways to use American ports in Maine instead.

The main grievance was the increases to railway freight rates that came about as a result of the integration of the Intercolonial Railway or ICR into the newly-nationalized Canadian National Railway (CNR). As a result, freight rates in the Maritimes immediately rose by 40%, later by over 100%. Maritimers pointed out that the ICR was part of the Confederation deal, that its long and uneconomic route resulted from decisions made by Ottawa, and that its main purpose was to support Maritime economic development and Canadian political integration. The arguments fell on deaf ears and Nova Scotian exports suffered a drastic decline because of the higher rates.

The Maritime Rights Movement also looked to provincial politics for support. There the Liberal government was ill-equipped to deal with the economic crisis. Premier Murray was replaced in 1923 by Ernest Armstrong who soon demonstrated a lack of judgment and leadership skills. The long-governing party was suspicious of new ideas, and clearly in the pocket of big business. It also saw itself as the junior partner of the national Liberal Party and made little effort to press MacKenzie King's Liberal government to deal with provincial grievances.

In the mid-1920s the Conservative Party began to show some life. Party elites thought that the former MP Edgar Nelson Rhodes might be the right person to lead the party to power as he was a superb speaker and a decent manager and organizer. One night the current leader, W. L. Hall, was beaten up, and the rumour was that a Black man had discovered him having an affair with his wife. The possibility of a sex and race scandal was too much for the Conservatives. He was forced to resign and Rhodes took over the party on the eve of the 1925 election. By then the Conservatives had adopted Maritime Rights as their political platform and were ready to fight the election on it.

In the summer of 1925 another violent strike broke out in Cape Breton. The company powerhouse at New Waterford was wrecked, buildings were burnt at Reserve Mines, and looting occurred at Glace Bay. BESCO police fired into an unarmed crowd killing one miner. BESCO tried to starve the workers into submission, a blunder that brought national support for the workers. In response the Conservatives organized relief for workers' families while the Liberal government continued to support BESCO. In these circumstances the election brought to an end the long Liberal dynasty. The Conservatives raised their popular vote from 25% to 61%, the highest popular vote in provincial history, increasing their seat total from three to 40. The Liberals lost 26 of their 29 seats, their worst showing in Nova Scotian history.

By 1926 Mackenzie King was back in power in Ottawa. He appointed a commission under Sir Andrew Duncan to examine the Maritime economy and recommend solutions. The Duncan Commission duly recommended that some adjustments be made to federal policies. The King government carefully calculated the minimum amount of concessions needed to divide, buy off, and weaken the political support for Maritime Rights without spending too much money or upsetting other regions of the country. The concessions included a 20% % reduction in freight rates, support for Halifax harbour, subsidies for coking plants using Cape Breton coal, and an increase in the federal subsidy of $875,000. In fact, the concessions were far less than they appeared. The railways applied the freight rate reductions to fewer commodities and shorter distances than expected. The subsidies were subject to conditions. Investment in Halifax harbor did not offset federal policies that favoured American ports. Having bragged of their success, the local politicians were in no position to complain once they read the details. The rest of Canada had no stomach for more complaints, and the Maritime Rights Movement withered away.

Attempting to grapple with the continuing depression was the new Conservative government of Edgar Rhodes. He brought in some long-overdue reforms such as pensions for teachers and allowances for widowed mothers. He abolished the Legislative Council which had long since failed to provide any useful function. More importantly the new government helped bring peace to the coal and steel industries of Cape Breton. Oddly, the Rhodes government implemented the correct economic policy for dealing with a depression, namely deficit financing. That policy ran against the grain of current economic and political orthodoxy which argued that no matter how serious a depression was, government should never spend more than it raised in taxes. For nine successive years the Conservatives ran deficits which eased the depression but did them no good politically.

Immediately after their 1925 defeat the Liberals began renewing leader-ship and policies and rebuilding their once invincible political machine. By 1928 Rhodes had achieved no more success wringing concessions out of Ottawa than his predecessors. Cuts to services, tax increases and deficit financing were all unpopular with the voters. Rhodes noted the Liberal resurgence and called an election to head off certain defeat. His instincts were sound - the Conservative vote dropped from 61% to 51% and their seat total from 40 to 23, the Liberals gaining three seats for a total of 20, their popular vote bouncing back from 36% to 48%.

Another of the major achievements of the Rhodes government was the partial abolition of prohibition. Nova Scotia was legally "dry," but a significant portion of the population continued to partake of alcohol. Rum running was a huge business with Nova Scotian schooners smuggling West Indian rum into the thousands of bays and coves along the coast. It was never illegal to manufac-ture liquor, and bootleggers found ways to obtain some of that product for the local market. Police and courts accepted bribes to turn a blind eye or drop charges. Liquor could be used legally for medicinal purposes and doctors will-ingly wrote thousands of prescriptions for dubious ailments. Prohibition was turning ordinary citizens into law breakers and undermining respect for the law, police, courts and government itself.

Following a plebiscite in October 1929 the Conservatives made it legal to buy liquor for consumption at home. They established the Nova Scotia Liquor Commission as a government monopoly so the government could cap-ture the huge profits the smugglers had been making. From then on the prohi-bitionists fought a rear-guard action delaying every attempt to liberalize liquor laws, making it impossible for wine and beer to be served in restaurants, pre-venting women from drinking in pubs, and pressuring government to impose heavy taxes to discourage consumption. One effect of the partial legalization of alcohol was an immediate jump in government revenue, and by 1940 liquor taxes constituted one-third of all provincial revenue. Another effect was that employment in government owned liquor stores and marketing to them became lucrative sources of patronage for the government in power. Step by timid step successive governments relaxed the restrictions, but many remained half a cen-tury later and it was always politically dangerous for a government to ease the restrictions on consuming alcohol.

In the late 1920s Nova Scotia's position showed signs of improvement. Economic growth elsewhere and Ottawa's half-hearted responses to the Duncan Commission stimulated demand for Nova Scotia's products. This brief period of optimism was cut short in 1929 when the Great Depression struck the province with full force. Within a year the value of agricultural production had declined by 40%, fish production by 47%, timber production by 75%, employment in the Halifax docks by 50% and employment in manufacturing by 40%. Unemployment surged to 20%. This time there was no escape to the United States which closed its borders to immigration, and by 1933 fully one-seventh of the population was on relief.

Municipal governments were soon overwhelmed with families seeking welfare. They responded to the crisis with minimal effort, refusing to support people rich enough to own homes, demanding proof that there was no independent source of income, sending inspectors to confirm the level of poverty, issuing coupons to buy cheap products in authorized stores, and humiliating those who asked for support. In spite of such restrictions municipalities were soon bankrupted by the growing demand. The province stepped in with matching grants, but that only helped municipalities with enough money to pay their share. Ottawa introduced a program requiring each level of government to pay one-third the cost but Nova Scotia could not afford to participate. Soon the 10% of Canada's population living in the Maritimes was only receiving 3.5% of federal spending on relief because the provincial and local governments couldn't match the federal contributions.

The provincial government encouraged people to re-settle abandoned farms. Those who did could grow food and cut wood for fuel, but re-settling such land just perpetrated a different form of poverty. Farmers spent more time fishing and cutting wood, and unemployed urban dwellers moved back to the family farm. The federal government set up work camps but it imposed such humiliation and strict discipline that men preferred to move from town to town begging for work or food. Restoring the Halifax Citadel was one such project, but conditions were so terrible that not all the potential jobs were filled.

To supplement the efforts of government private citizens, charities, church groups and others provided tents and soup kitchens. The Antigonish Movement encouraged fishermen and farmers to form cooperatives and had positive effects on marketing, quality control and the psychological benefits of doing something to make things better. It could not, however, compensate for the fact that the markets simply were not there. Throughout this decade-long crisis governments and elites and those with jobs persisted in the belief that jobs really were available and that workers were just too fussy or lazy to take them.

In 1930 Premier Rhodes joined the federal government, and was replaced by Gordon Harrington, MLA for Glace Bay. As Minister of Labour, Harrington had brought peace to industrial Cape Breton. More progressive than either Rhodes or the provincial Liberal Party, he was a genuine reformer with the interests of ordinary workers at heart. He could not, however, defeat the Depression and with revenue falling he was forced to cut back on popular programs.

BESCO, whose management had been so disastrous, had been succeeded by the Dominion Steel and Coal Corporation or DOSCO. By 1931 falling demand for coal led its management to insist that the miners take a 12% cut in pay. The United Mine Workers rejected the proposal. Premier Harrington appointed a commission to head off a strike and obtained a federal subsidy which should have increased sales by one million tons. But demand still fell short, the commission supported wage cuts, and some collieries were closed. The UMW reluctantly accepted the wage cut, but in 1933 DOSCO went into receivership threatening 3,200 workers with unemployment.

In 1933 the Conservatives tried to avoid defeat with a blatant attempt to rig the election. A new process provided that voters' lists would be prepared by regulators rather than municipal governments. However, only three regulators were appointed for the whole of Halifax. The Liberals demanded that more be appointed and took the matter to court where the judge appointed 40 regulators. When the lists were posted, sometimes in the most inaccessible of locations or late at night, people discovered that thousands of known voters were no longer on the roll. The blatant attempt at manipulation degenerated into farce when grey-haired seniors were asked for proof they were old enough to vote.

In 1930 the Liberals met to select a new leader from among some unimpressive candidates. To everyone's surprise one delegate nominated Angus L. Macdonald. He reluctantly accepted the nomination and won on the first ballot. Macdonald was a Scottish Catholic from Inverness who had excelled at studies and athletics at St. Francis Xavier University, Dalhousie and Harvard. He was charming, clever, and a gifted orator. He was also ambitious and extremely hard-working, and assiduously cultivated the image of an honest Scottish chieftain.

Macdonald immediately threw himself into preparing for the next election, touring the province, building the party, attracting candidates, and lining up party workers and finances. The Liberals romped home with 22 seats, a gain of two in an Assembly now reduced to 30 members because of the Depression. The Conservatives lost 15 seats falling to eight. The popular vote was not so dramatic, with the Conservatives losing only 5% of the vote to the Liberals in spite of the Depression, a new Liberal leader and platform, and the unpopularity of both provincial and federal Conservatives. Macdonald became the first Catholic to be elected premier of Nova Scotia, and he quickly proved that religion and politics could be separated to the annoyance of the Catholic hierarchy which expected favourable treatment. On the day he assumed office he began creating the legend of Angus L. Macdonald.

Chapter Nine

Angus L.Macdonald, 1933-1954

On 5 September 1933 Angus L. Macdonald became premier of Nova Scotia. Apart from service in Ottawa during World War II, he would govern the province until his death in 1954, one of the most popular, loved and respected of its many premiers. On the first day of his new administration he honoured the campaign promise to include Nova Scotia in the federal old age pension program, and other promises were quickly fulfilled such as providing free school texts to students up to grade IX.

Macdonald believed that it was harmful to one's character to receive welfare. Instead he launched a massive, labour-intensive program of road building and paving. Part of that program was financed by reducing the amount of money the gas companies received and raising the provincial gas tax by two cents per gallon. By 1937 there were 600 kilometres of paved road, up from less than 50 in 1933, and this doubled by 1939. Another highly successful program was subsidizing electricity lines in rural areas which improved the lives of a large portion of the province's population.

Another priority was labour relations in the coal industry. Macdonald incorporated the views of labour, the Conservative opposition and the latest American laws into one of the most advanced labour laws of the day. That law made it illegal for companies to dismiss workers for organizing unions, required companies to collect union dues from all employees (compulsory check-off), and required companies to bargain with any union chosen by a majority of its employees.

The promotion of tourism was a major thrust of governmental policy. Hotels and restaurants were given loans and their staffs were given training. The Cape Breton Highlands National Park was established with a modern resort and golf course. Visitors driving into the province were met by a bagpiper in full Highland dress. Heritage was emphasized in promotional leaflets that showed happy Scots, Irish and French people in traditional dress maintaining their unique culture of music and games.

The Liberals were obsessed with balancing the provincial budget and Macdonald cut spending ruthlessly. The deficit fell quickly, mainly because the economy began to improve. Macdonald underestimated revenue and overestimated expenditure so that every year he could take credit for good management. The lower spending on welfare slashed the deficit while increased expenditure on road paving was charged to the capital account. The result was that every year the "operating budget" came closer to being balanced while the province actually sank deeper into debt. In this way in 1937 Macdonald was able to announce the first budgetary surplus in 14 years.

Another promise that Macdonald honoured was to establish a commission to examine the economy. The terms of reference pointed the commission towards the answers the government expected. The commission's report highlighted the usual complaints about high federal tariffs, a discriminatory federal transportation policy, and inadequate federal subsidies. As usual the federal government did nothing about them. Macdonald acted on a few recommendations that were within provincial power and cost little, such as setting up an advisory council on economic policy, but he ignored others such creating a more professional civil service.

On the major issues Macdonald had done as promised and he called an election for 29 July 1937. This time he ran on his record and made no new promises. There was no change in the popular vote but the Liberals gained two seats. After the election Macdonald turned his attention to federal politics. Mackenzie King had appointed a Royal Commission to determine whether a rearrangement of federal and provincial responsibilities and taxation fields might mitigate some of the suffering. Macdonald certainly thought so and threw himself into drafting Nova Scotia's brief. He proposed that Ottawa take full responsibility for unemployment insurance, old-age pensions, and mothers' allowances - after years of debate Ottawa did assume responsibility for unemployment insurance. Macdonald also argued that the federal government should redistribute wealth from the richer to the poorer provinces so that standards of service would be comparable across the country. He continued to fight for such "equalization payments" throughout his career and helped pave the way for their acceptance in 1955.

Canada went to war against Germany on 10 September 1939 and Nova Scotians again volunteered by the tens of thousands. Others supported the war effort through voluntary organizations that provided supplies, funds, assistance for the families of enlisted men and women, food and entertainment for the troops, and guards for dams and power stations. Mackenzie King recruited Macdonald for the federal cabinet, and he was immediately replaced by Highways Minister A.S. MacMillan. Macmillan was an excellent choice, a strong, experienced, and popular minister because of his successful management of the roads program and rural electrification. He provided the province with competent if unspectacular government during the war. Macmillan called an election for 28 October 1941 in the face of growing support for the Co-operative Commonwealth Federation (CCF), a coalition of labour, farmers and socialists. The Liberals held their popular vote of 52.7% but lost two seats winning a total of 22. The Conservatives fell from 46% to 40% of the popular vote winning five seats. The CCF was indeed on the march, winning its first three seats.

Once more Halifax became one of the most important ports on the Atlantic coast, and its importance grew dramatically during the war. Unemployment disappeared, labour shortages developed, and businesses welcomed the first signs of prosperity since 1918. Britain was soon dependent on North America for its supplies, and most of them passed through Halifax. The RCAF established or expanded bases in Sydney, Debert, Yarmouth and Shelburne, and thousands of air force personnel were trained at the British Commonwealth Air Training base at Greenwood.

Halifax was the natural port for ship repair and shipbuilding. In 1940, however, the federal government decided to build up the industrial capacity of central Canada by concentrating shipbuilding in the St. Lawrence-Great Lakes region. Those facilities, however, could not be fully utilized in winter and the policy was reversed a year later. Though the Halifax shipyards were soon working 24 hours a day they could not meet the demand, and the construction and repair of smaller vessels was transferred to Sydney, Lunenburg, Liverpool, and Bridgewater. During the war only 6% of Canadian shipbuilding was done in the Maritmes, an absurd situation given its natural advantage.

As German submarines sank merchant shipping it was again clear that the only safe way to cross the Atlantic was in convoys, and the place to assemble them was Halifax. Halifax became a gigantic hotel housing tens of thousands of enlisted men waiting for embarkation and equal numbers of sailors and merchant mariners waiting for their convoys to be assembled. The city hadn't fully recovered from World War I, the Halifax explosion and two decades of depression, and before the war even began it had serious shortages in every branch of infrastructure – housing, hotels, streets, water and sewage, transportation, bridges and entertainment.

The arrival of additional military personnel strained facilities to the limit. Halls and church basements were turned into emergency hostels, tents sprouted in the parks, and instant wartime housing was erected. Due to rationing private citizens and businessmen could not build additional facilities or obtain adequate supplies. Having experienced two decades of Depression, property owners now charged whatever rent the traffic would bear. Services like hospitals and public transportation were completely overwhelmed. There were only nine cinemas, and people had to queue for hours for any kind of entertainment. The highly-restrictive liquor laws further limited the possibilities for relaxation and entertainment. Church and charitable groups made a massive effort to accommodate the armed forces with socials, dinners, dances and entertainment but the city experienced a rapid change in social mores, and drinking, prostitution and bootlegging thrived.

City and provincial authorities pointed out to Ottawa that in making Halifax the centre of Maritime operations the federal government had created a social and economic crisis not experienced by any other city. Ottawa, they argued, should do something to help the municipal government deal with the crisis. Ottawa's answer was that all cities faced problems. The provincial government did not take advantage of the boom to raise taxes and it still attached the highest priority to balancing the budget. It did little to help Halifax, a fact Ottawa would certainly have noticed when the province asked for assistance.

The provincial government saw its prime duty as supporting the war effort, and introduced very little legislation during the war. Financing the war was a national challenge, and the federal government's proposed solution was to allow Ottawa to collect most forms of taxation during the war. That would avoid duplication with the provinces, create uniform standards, make evasion difficult, and produce adequate federal revenues to fight the war. In return for vacating these taxation fields the provinces would receive per capita grants larger than what they could have collected themselves. MacMillan had very grave doubts about the plan because it threatened to emasculate provincial autonomy, but to object would be unpatriotic and Nova Scotia reluctantly signed on.

Throughout the war more and more soldiers and sailors were stationed in Halifax increasing the pressure on all facilities. Resentment against landlords and store owners mounted. When victory over Germany was announced on 7 May 1945, 8,000 sailors were on shore leave with hardly any restaurants open to entertain them and the jubilant crowds. At 10.30 pm some sailors burned a tram on Barrington Street. Civilians joined the demonstration and soon they broke into liquor stores and into Keith's brewery. They were soon celebrating in the streets and parks, their instant parties often degenerating into drunken orgies. All night long roving mobs broke windows, stole goods and damaged property. The following morning thousands more servicemen joined in. By the time the navy cancelled shore leave later that day, two sailors were dead, 17 people were injured, 250 had been arrested and close to 600 stores had been damaged. Most people believed that the riot reflected widespread anger over years of gouging, but an investigation found the military authorities responsible for failing to take measures to control their personnel.

At war's end Macdonald came back to reclaim the premiership. He immediately called an election for 23 October 1945 on the slogan "Angus L's Back" and won an overwhelming mandate of 28 out of 30 seats. For the first time since Confederation the Conservatives elected no MLAs. The CCF won two seats on a 13.6% share of the vote which made them the official opposition. Though Angus L. was back, wartime responsibilities had exhausted him and he had become increasingly conservative and cautious. He remained enormously popular but he was not ready to tackle post-war problems and issues.

Once more Macdonald's top priority was federal-provincial relations. Mackenzie King's goal was to convince the provinces to renew the wartime fiscal agreements so the federal government could shift defence spending to new social programs which were constitutionally provincial. Macdonald was totally opposed. He asserted that if the federal government continued to collect almost all taxes in peacetime, it would ultimately control almost all expenditures. Canada would become a centralized state and provincial jurisdiction would become almost meaningless. He argued that provinces should have exclusive jurisdiction over taxes on gasoline, electricity, and amusement, items the federal government had not taxed before the war. He articulated this position at the federal-provincial conferences in 1945 and 1946. Ontario and Quebec agreed, and the conference rejected King's proposal.

King's response was to make separate agreements with each province beginning with the poorer ones. Macdonald denounced the policy as destructive of federalism because it would create a patchwork of fiscal regimes and foster unfairness and envy between provinces. Ottawa offered the poorer provinces attractive arrangements and one by one they agreed. Macdonald was successful in getting the federal government to leave some tax fields exclusively within provincial jurisdiction, and he finally signed the agreement. He had forced Ottawa to enrich its offer, and Nova Scotia found itself with large budgetary surpluses in the late 1940s. Macdonald used some of that revenue plus rapidly growing income from liquor sales to finance more road building, rural electrification, and an ambitious program of school building. However, he also continued to pay down the provincial debt instead of addressing the increasing crisis in municipal services.

Another of the battles Macdonald lost was over freight rates. In 1948 the federal Board of Transport Commissioners proposed a 21% increase that would fall mainly on eastern and western Canada and potentially bankrupt even more of the faltering industries and businesses in the Maritimes. At a federal-provincial conference seven enraged premiers led by Macdonald pointed out that the formula used by the Board was seriously flawed. The federal government rejected their arguments but did make a few small adjustments. The Board then recommended a further 20% increase, and the furious premiers again demanded federal intervention.

The federal government appointed a royal commission that concluded the rate increases were generally acceptable. Between 1947 and 1953 Maritime freight rates almost doubled, a clear defeat for Macdonald and another blow to the Nova Scotia economy. Macdonald's tactics may help explain why he lost so many of his battles with Ottawa. No matter how little the province received from Ottawa, Macdonald threw the entire weight of the provincial Liberal party behind the federal Liberals in every election. Macdonald's pressure on Ottawa consisted mainly of sending reports and letters instead of making the federal Liberals pay a political price for ignoring Nova Scotia.

In 1949 Macdonald called another election with his government running on the slogan "All's Well with Angus L." It was a catchy and clever slogan because it put the focus squarely on the party's greatest asset, but it was an inaccurate description of the state of affairs. Macdonald himself was not well. He was still a chain-smoking work addict, and his superb mastery of issues came at a price to his health. He was more capable than any of his ministers and more knowledgeable about their departments and his inability to delegate undermined them. He was always very cautious and conservative, traits now turning into procrastination.

The province itself was far from well. Major industries such as fishing, agriculture, forestry and mining were all in relative decline. Macdonald's government had gradually sided with industry against unions. That allowed industry to deal with its increasingly uncompetitive situation by forcing down wages instead of investing in new technology and paying higher salaries to fewer workers. While that policy reduced unemployment, it meant that more people were earning less relative to the rest of Canada. While Canada's gross domestic product grew 100% in the decade after World War II, Nova Scotia's only grew by two-thirds as much.

The fishery industry offered one of the best examples of decline. Traditionally fishermen had gone to sea in their own boats and sold their catch to the processing companies. The fishermen were considered "co-adventurers", and the selling price was divided 40% to the fishermen and 60% to the companies. The system worked to the advantage of the companies because they set the selling price, and fishermen found themselves amongst the poorest people in the province. Technology changed in the 1920s with the arrival of trawlers that could operate at reduced cost all year long, a change that would produce fewer higher-paying jobs. In order to protect jobs in the fishery, however, the Nova Scotian government opposed the licensing of trawlers for decades, driving down fishermen's income.

After World War II the pressure grew to modernize by using more trawlers. The men who worked on them were clearly employees of the big companies and hence entitled to unionize. Some inshore fishermen decided that they too should unionize. In 1946 they organized the Canadian Fishermen and Fish Handlers' Union or CFFU, and went on strike on 26 December. The companies fought the strike with every tactic available, including smearing union leaders with charges that they were Communist. Some were, and the tactic proved highly effective. American unions were invited in to help break the local ones, and goons were used to intimidate fishermen. On the legal front the courts sided with the companies; on the political side the government's Trade Union Act of 1947 also weakened the unions.

The decline in the shipping industry was also accelerated by poor federal policies and labour problems. Canada emerged from the war with one of the largest shipping fleets in the world, much of it based in Nova Scotia. The federal government then decided to sell it off, and between 1943 and 1950 employment in maritime shipping fell from 75,000 to 12,000. The industry also suffered from problems with labour. In 1948 Canadian shipping companies were under pressure from the Canadian Seamen's Union or CSU to grant better wages and conditions. The companies invited the American Seafarer's International Union, the SIU, to break the strike. In March 1949 the SIU sent 200 thugs to take over a ship being picketed by a dozen CSU men engaged in a legal strike. The strike-breakers fired on the picketers injuring eight of them. The next morning other seamen walked off in a sympathy strike, and 4,000 people marched on City Hall to protest the unprovoked violence. The CSU leaders were accused of being Communists and their strike was broken. The Macdonald government, which had pioneered advanced labour legislation in 1937, stood idly by.

Other problems beset the province in the post-World War II environment. The lucrative United Kingdom market for apples could not be recaptured and a mainstay of the economy of the Annapolis Valley was severely restricted. Agriculture continued to decline with fewer farms and low incomes, harming the towns and villages that serviced agricultural areas. The forestry industry stagnated, with small woodlot owners eking out a poor living selling pulpwood to the big paper companies. Coal mining continued its steady decline due to the switchover to diesel, oil, and hydroelectricity. More industries closed and young people continued to migrate elsewhere.

The government had no policies specifically designed to attract new industry. It continued to pour subsidies into coal mines which slowed the loss of jobs but could not make them productive. In effect, it was investing in yesterday's industries rather than in the future. One example was the coal mine in Macdonald's own constituency of Inverness which the government ran from 1934 to 1951 at a total loss of millions of dollars.

Still "All's Well with Angus L." seemed a good slogan to fight the 1949 election. The Liberals were in excellent shape financially. Some of that money came from brewers, distillers, and wineries that contributed to the Liberal Party to ensure that their products were sold in the government-owned liquor stores. Another lucrative source of party funds was the bottle exchange which bought empty beer bottles and sold them back to the breweries, much of the profit going to the party. Nevertheless, Macdonald won only the same number of seats although the size of the Assembly had increased from 30 to 37. The Progressive Conservatives under Robert Stanfield returned to respectability with 39.2% of the popular vote and seven seats.

After the election, federal-provincial conflicts continued to dominate Macdonald's political agenda. The next battle was over pensions. A federal-provincial conference reached agreement on a shared-cost program that provided pensions for those with incomes of under $600 per year. When announcing the program, however, Ottawa said the income ceiling would be $720. That raised Nova Scotia's share of the payments, meaning that the federal government was making decisions on how a province should spend its own money. A furious Macdonald said there was no point in having federal-provincial conferences if Ottawa then announced decisions in violation of the agreement it had just reached.

These setbacks and problems did not affect Macdonald's standing with the public because he was seen as having done the best he could to protect the province's rights and interests. They also came at a time of increasing prosperity. By 1949 the Cold War was well underway and the Korean War soon broke out. This time Ottawa spent large amounts of money in Halifax, and the entire province was swept up in the general boom of the 1950s. The fact that the rest of Canada was growing faster did not seem to bother people who were, for the first time, acquiring cars, household appliances, holidays, and possibly new homes in the suburbs of Halifax. Progress could also be seen as two of Macdonald's infrastructure mega projects neared completion, namely the bridge over Halifax harbor that bears his name and the Canso Causeway that eliminated the ferry ride between Cape Breton and the mainland.

In these circumstances Macdonald called an election for 1953. He was growing more cautious and domineering in contrast to Conservative leader Stanfield who was becoming more confident and popular. Stanfield effectively criticized the Liberals on a number of issues including the lack of an industrial policy, lack of support for the municipalities, over-spending on schools and under-spending on roads, corruption, and failure to deal with the decline of the coal industry. Macdonald's usual answer – that the Conservatives had provided poor government two decades earlier – sounded increasingly irrelevant. The Liberal vote dropped below 50% while the Conservatives gained another 4% for 43.4%. The Liberals lost five seats to the Conservatives, the CCF holding its two seats while its popular vote continued to decline.

Then on 13 April 1954 Angus L. died of a heart attack at age 63. The province went into mourning and an estimated 100,000 people paid their respects. He had dominated the province for two decades. The booming and modern province economy of the 1950s could hardly be compared to that of 1933 when he became premier, and Angus L. was credited with much of that transition. He had become a political legend, the clan chieftain looking after his people, and he was respected, loved and admired for his qualities and achievements.

Chapter Ten

The Stanfield Years, 1954-1970

In the mid-50s three developments changed the political, economic and social history of Nova Scotia. One was an act of political suicide by the provincial Liberal regime that had governed since 1933. Another was the resurgence of the provincial Conservatives, and the final development of a viable two-party system. The third was the acceptance by the federal government that it had a responsibility to re-distribute wealth from richer to poorer parts of the country.

Angus L. Macdonald's death forced a leadership contest on the Liberal party. It was unfair for one of the candidates to be interim leader and hence premier. The front runner was Harold Connolly, but he preferred to retire to the comforts of the Senate. That made him the perfect candidate for interim leader, and he promised not to run for the leadership. For some inexplicable reason, however, the federal Liberals delayed the announcement. Fearful of losing both jobs, Connolly decided to run for the provincial leadership, violating his promise and infuriating the other candidates.

Connolly, an Irish Catholic, was the most popular of the six candidates. One of his nominators, however, urged all Catholics to support him, making religion a factor in a party and a province where the Protestants represented two-thirds the voters. Nevertheless, Connolly almost won on the first ballot. The last candidate dropped out, but on the second ballot most of his votes went to Henry Hicks. Connolly continued to lead on the third, fourth and fifth ballot, but Hicks finally won on the sixth. Catholics declared that it was a Protestant conspiracy; Connolly refused to serve in Hicks' cabinet; and Catholic Liberals began deserting the party.

Hicks had been an extremely able minister. He was energetic, progressive, highly intelligent and hard working. He was also arrogant, impatient and lacking in judgment. Instead of reconciling the Catholics he called three by-elections to reinforce his leadership. The one that mattered was Halifax South because it had been Macdonald's seat and the Conservatives had to win seats in Halifax and in Catholic areas if they hoped to win an election. Both parties poured massive resources into the contest, but the Conservatives won.

Hicks wanted to put a more progressive stamp on the party and the province. One of his first initiatives was to cooperate with the other Maritime Premiers in creating the Atlantic Provinces Economic Council or APEC. Its goal was to sponsor studies of problems and to promote solutions, coordination and common positions for dealing with Ottawa. Another initiative was to reduce the amount of patronage and what the Conservatives called corruption. Far more important was Hicks' reforms of the education system. Nova Scotia had fallen far behind other provinces, and Hicks set out to consolidate rural schools, build schools, improve the quality of teaching and modernize curricula. All of these were necessary and good, but they were also expensive. Hicks greatly increased the province's financial contribution, but the municipalities also had to raise taxes, especially those that had been paying far less than their fair share.

In the last years of Macdonald's dynasty the Conservative party began to show signs of life. Robert Stanfield from the prominent business family in Truro began to take an interest in it, mainly because he believed that the province should have an effective opposition party. He began working to build the party, encourage people to join it, start some debate on policy, and re-build constituency organizations. Stanfield did not want to be the leader, but increasingly members of the leaderless party started to think that maybe he was their best bet. They started to see that his obvious political liabilities – terrible speaking style, awkwardness, and shyness – might be outweighed by his obvious qualities – intelligence, sincerity, honesty, dedication, patience, caution, and a philosophy of hope, optimism and hard work. Besides, he was independently wealthy and the party could not afford to pay its leader. In 1948 the party elected him as leader and in the 1949 election the Progressive Conservatives went from zero to seven seats, adding another five in the 1953 election.

Having put his stamp on the party with some overdue reforms, Hicks called an election for 30 October 1956. The Liberals should have won and almost certainly would have under Macdonald. Hicks had never reconciled the Catholics, and his education reforms created unpopular tax increases. His partial reform of fund-raising backfired. Hicks dismissed a few of the agents who handled kickbacks from liquor sales, indicating that there was some corruption. He then refused to make public a list Stanfield sent him naming more such agents because doing so would have infuriated party workers. Hicks also lost a debate over the key issue of building and paving roads, a program the Liberals had used successfully in every election since 1937. These debates left the impression that Hicks did not have a clear agenda, did not understand the details of government programs, and had very questionable political judgment.

The election was the closest in Nova Scotian history to that time. The Conservatives won 46.6% of the popular vote to 42.2% for the Liberals. On Cape Breton the Conservatives took five seats from the Liberals, giving Stanfield 24 seats to Hick's 18. In the rest of Nova Scotia a few hundred more votes in close constituencies would have re-elected the Liberals. Two factors decided the election – the Liberals loss of Catholic votes especially on Cape

Breton and the view of coal miners that the Conservatives could do more for them than either the Liberals had done or the CCF could do.

Stanfield's election came at a time when the federal government had begun to change its attitude towards the Maritimes. For the first time since Confederation Ottawa accepted that since its policies led to a concentration of industry and wealth in central Canada, it therefore had an obligation to redistribute some of that wealth to the poorer provinces so they could maintain services closer to the national Canadian average. The first of the so-called equalization grants came in the 1955 budget of the federal Liberal government.

That important step turned into a revolutionary change when John Diefenbaker led the federal Conservatives to victory in 1957 ending 22 years of Liberal domination. Diefenbaker won only seven more seats than the Liberals. His margin of victory came from an increase from five to 21 sets in the Maritimes, partly due to the support of Stanfield. Diefenbaker came from northern Saskatchewan, and shared the Maritime belief that Confederation had been unfair to eastern and western Canada. He also led the first government in which MPs from those regions outnumbered central Canadian MPs.

The result was a flood of programs designed to reduce the disparity in income, standard of living and opportunity between the Maritimes and the rest of the country. The federal government increased the equalization grants and launched a series of programs to subsidize power, freight rates and coal production, to encourage new industry, to build infrastructure, and to support rural development. Tourism received a boost with the restoration of Louisbourg and the development of Cape Breton Highlands National Park. The new policy was made permanent by being institutionalized with the Atlantic Development Board and other federal departments and organizations.

In these circumstances Stanfield set out to put Nova Scotia's house in order so it could contribute as a full partner to economic development. Immediately after the election he faced the pent-up demand of party workers for a purge of the civil service and the appointment of good Conservatives. Stanfield told them they would get re-elected if they provided good governance, and for the first time since 1847 civil servants were not dismissed following a change of government. Stanfield also reformed government contracting. No company that received such contracts could contribute to the party, and no contract could go to a Conservative company if that meant increased costs. The government kept a list of qualified companies, the lowest tender got the contract, and the connection between contracts and support for the party was broken.

The new Conservative government began fulfilling is promises with expanded road building and paving, an accelerated pace of school consolidation, the construction of technical and vocational schools, increased funding for education and health, and the teaching French up to grade XII. The provincial government finally began providing massive financial support to the universities. It entered the federal-provincial hospital insurance plan and later the Medicare program. It took further steps to end prohibition, allowing restaurants to serve been and wine. It intervened directly in the economy with the revitalization of downtown Halifax and legislation that prevented a company based outside the province, Bell Canada, from taking over the Maritime Telegraph and Telephone Company. Stanfield pursued all his proposals through consensus, one aspect being closer cooperation with other governments in Atlantic Canada and especially with the federal government.

For a decade Stanfield had criticized the government for its laissez-faire approach to the economy. Stanfield believed that passive philosophy combined with decades of relative economic stagnation and the migration of the young and energetic had created a population that accepted the inevitability of low incomes and limited opportunities. He believed Nova Scotians had become pessimists and whiners, willing to ask Ottawa for help, unwilling to take action themselves. He set out to change that attitude in both government and the public. His government would end complacency and take initiatives and actions to attract industry, create jobs, produce taxes, raise the standard of living, teach Nova Scotians that they could become a viable part of the Canadian economy, and restore pride and confidence.

His main instrument was Industrial Estates Limited or IEL, created in 1957. It was managed by a group of prominent and successful businessmen under the direction of Frank Sobey. It was initially given $12 million in government funding, but was independent of government influence. Its mandate was to attract new industries to the province by providing buildings, capital, and other incentives. Decisions were made by the board of directors chosen from the leading businessmen of the province, decisions based on business principles and not political considerations. At the time it was an innovative departure from government's traditional role in economic development, and indeed put Nova Scotia in the forefront of such development in Canada.

IEL immediately set out to attract industry, and within years had helped over 50 companies locate their businesses in the province, companies that created some 12,000 jobs directly or indirectly. These included car assembly plants in Sydney and Dartmouth, a fish processing plant in Lunenburg, a carpet mill in Truro, and a hardboard plant in Chester. Its greatest achievement was in attracting the Michelin tire plant to Dartmouth, followed by two more such plants. Michelin became one of largest employers in the province, accounted for one half the growth in employment in the early 1970s. By then IEL had helped reverse the relative decline that Nova Scotia had experienced since Confederation, and between 1956 and 1971 Nova Scotia's per capita income increased from 72% to 78% of the Canadian national average.

In spite of these successes IEL was a high-risk operation and one-third of its projects failed. Its main weaknesses were an over-eagerness to attract investment because of the need to create jobs, and a lack of expertise to evaluate proposals in terms of cost, market, management or technology. These weaknesses would lead to two spectacular failures which ultimately led to the demise of IEL and of the Conservative government that created it.

IEL and Stanfield thought it had executed a coup when it attracted Clairtone Sound Corporation, a rapidly-growing manufacturer of hi-tech stereo equipment. IEL provided $8,000,000 and the factory in Stellarton was soon employing 1,000 workers. Almost as soon as the factory opened, however, Clairtone profits began to shrink, and it soon became clear that the owners were experts at marketing rather than management. Nevertheless, IEL continued with the project, even when Clairtone decided to enter the emerging market for colour TVs without any expertise in the area. That mistake soon produced huge losses, and in 1967 IEL took over the company. By the time the factory closed in 1970 it had probably cost the taxpayers over $13,000,000.

Far worse was IEL's misadventure with the heavy water plant at Glace Bay. Atomic Energy of Canada (AECL) needed a secure supply of heavy water for its Candu nuclear reactors. Only two companies had the technology to supply that demand, one being an American organization owned by Jerome Spevack. It created a Canadian subsidiary known as Deutronium of Canada Limited or DCL. IEL offered to support it, and DCL won the AECL contract. That contract committed DCL to supply heavy water at a fixed price, but all IEL knew about the cost of production was a rough estimate that the new plant would cost $30 million. Spevack was to provide $18 million and be in control, IEL was to provide $12 million and be a silent partner. Cape Breton would get 200 permanent jobs in the plant, 500 jobs in the coal mines which would provide the fuel, and 2,000 short-term jobs during construction. The proposal was extremely attractive, partly because it would put Nova Scotia on the cutting edge of nuclear technology instead of the dying side of coal and steel.

The federal government then decided that DCL had to be Canadian owned, leaving Nova Scotia the choice of taking ownership or losing the project. Without any knowledge of heavy water and without any capacity for management, IEL took ownership but left DCL in charge of building and running the plant. DCL then found it impossible to raise its $18 million share of the cost, and IEL had to put up the entire investment of $30,000,000 while still using DCL as builder and manager. Though neither AECL, DCL nor IEL actually knew if the plant could produce heavy water at the agreed price, AECL doubled its order. That sounded like even more of a good thing, and IEL agreed to double the size of the plant, its investment now estimated at $87 million.

Construction was plagued by official and unofficial strikes, and completion dates were postponed as cost estimates escalated. A decision was taken to use salt water for cooling on the mistaken grounds that it would be less expensive. Somehow the salt water system was not properly maintained and the stainless steel pipes corroded. Ultimately the plant never produced heavy water, and IEL and the Nova Scotian government lost over $100 million on a project that they never understood. Oddly, the federal government then reversed its decision regarding Canadian ownership and allowed foreign-owned General Electric of Canada to build a heavy water plant at Port Hawkesbury, which was quite successful.

Fortunately for Stanfield these disasters came to fruition after he left the province. By then he had become one of the province's most popular and successful politicians ever. He was highly respected for his honesty and integrity, for the success of his policies, for his willingness to take risks to reverse the relative decline of his province. He ran his government and his province by consensus, floating ideas, making proposals, listening to the feedback, altering or postponing proposals until there was general support. He was also helped by the general economic boom of the 1960s and by continued generosity from Ottawa, including that of the Liberal Government that replaced Diefenbaker in 1964. With these advantages Stanfield won re-election in 1960 with 27 seats, in 1963 with 39 seats, and in 1967 with 40 out of 46 seats.

A few months later Stanfield won the leadership of the federal Progressive Conservative party. He was replaced without a convention by his ablest lieutenant, Ike Smith. Smith had compensated Stanfield's weaknesses and reinforced his strengths. He was smart, hard-working, well-organized, and the best speaker and debater in the party. He was an excellent minister and a team player, but he was not able to delegate and he concentrated on details rather than on managing the government and the province. Smith carried on with Stanfield's policies, but he ran into severe bad luck.

Almost immediately after assuming office Smith faced a crisis that had been brewing for decades. DOSCO announced that it would close its steel plant in Sydney. The announcement was met with rage because for years DOSCO had been running down its plant, transferring the profitable assets elsewhere, and demanding and receiving support from all three levels of government on the threat of closure. It has obtained that support, and now it was closing the plant anyway. The provincial government immediately took over the plant hoping to find a commercial buyer.

Smith called an election for 13 October 1970. Unfortunately he appeared old at 61 while Liberal leader Gerald Regan was young at 41. Regan had been making frantic accusations against the government for years, and they had an effect especially as the DCL fiasco unfolded. The election was the closest in Nova Scotian history. The Conservatives actually outvoted the Liberals 47% to 46 %. But in Cape Breton the workers turned their backs on the government that had just saved their jobs at DOSCO, and that switch of votes from Conservatives to Liberals and NDP made the difference. Regan found himself with 23 MLAs to Smith's 21, and formed a minority government with the support of the New Democratic Party. As in 1956, a change of leader had cost the governing party an election, and even the Liberals said that Stanfield would have won.

The Stanfield era brought an extremely important change to Nova Scotian politics, namely the replacement of one-party rule by the Liberals with a genuine two party system in which the parties rotate in office every decade or so. Prior to 1955 the Liberals had been in office for all but 12 years since Confederation. While they provided relatively decent and scandal-free government during that period, one party rule proved unhealthy for both democracy and the economy. Safe Liberal governments ignored major issues that required spending political capital or taking risk, and they grew complacent. Faced with the prospect of losing election after election, the opposition found it hard to attract good candidates and became, like the government, a risk-avoider rather than a source of new ideas and proposals. The CCF-NDP was the party of new ideas, but the public preferred the "old-line" parties.

Examples of the harmful effects of one-party rule abound in the history of the province. The Liberals avoided introducing essential reforms to municipal government, and when the Conservatives did they were defeated in the next election. For decades the province suffered from a lack of government investment in infrastructure, but the government's main response was to ask Ottawa for more money. Federal subsidies were indeed inadequate, but one reason Ottawa was not sympathetic after Confederation was that Ontario and Quebec collected property taxes to pay for education while Nova Scotian governments did not.

The Liberals under Macdonald, Macmillan and Hicks were extremely successful politically from 1934 to 1955. During that period Nova Scotia continued to complain about its status within Confederation and to ask Ottawa for increased grants. Unlike the Ontario and Quebec governments, however, that Liberal government did not collect corporate and income taxes. That undoubtedly prolonged one-party rule but it hardly encouraged the rest of Canada to subsidize social services in Nova Scotia. Macdonald's legacy included balancing the budget during the Depression when people were almost starving, failure to help Halifax deal with the infrastructure crisis of World War II, failure to invest in new industries, and failure to raise taxes that were within provincial jurisdiction. One-party domination was, in fact, one of the major reasons Nova Scotia fell farther and farther behind the rest of Canada after Confederation.

Stanfield entered politics because he recognized that one-party rule was extremely harmful. At the time the Conservatives had no seats at all in the Assembly and there was very little effective criticism of government policies and actions. His first message was that the province needed an effective opposition. His second message was that the province had to change its attitude, that second-class services were not good enough, that Nova Scotians could succeed, that the province and its government had to take initiatives and risks and stop waiting for outsiders to solve their problems. Stanfield's asked Ottawa to supplement efforts the province was making, not to assume responsibility for the province's problems.

Stanfield's regime stands out from the previous regimes because he did take courageous decisions and risks. That also meant that unlike the regimes of Fielding, Murray and Macdonald, his party was vulnerable to public backlash when some of those risks failed. Stanfield actually created a two-party system both deliberately and inadvertently. He deliberately wore the liberals down and replaced them in 1955. He then did not follow the one-party path of avoiding risk and begging Ottawa for grants or blaming others for the provinces failures. That meant that his successor, Ike Smith, went into the 1970 election with the responsibility for the both the successes and failures of the Stanfield years squarely on his shoulders, and he lost that election.

The newly-elected Liberals of Gerald Regan followed more in the footsteps of Stanfield than of Macdonald, Murray and Fielding. They took risks, made mistakes and failed to re-create the safe, easy, comfortable ways of the one-party regimes of the past. Regan was defeated in 1978 by John Buchanan who also governed more in the manner of Stanfield than of Macdonald, and governed for only 12 years. In effect, from 1955 on the province has had a genuine choice in each election, and it has used those opportunities to change governments five times. No government since the 1950s has been able to take re-election for granted, and the main opposition party has know that it has a real chance of winning if it works hard enough. Since the 1950s the new attitudes of both the provincial and federal governments have produced sustained investment in industry, business and governmental services. Nova Scotia has regained the status it held before Confederation as a proud, productive, and confident partner in British North America.

Nova Scotia has a long and distinguished history which, paradoxically and unfortunately, has not been reflected in any great outpouring of provincial history texts. It was that lacunae, in fact, which provided the original motivation for writing this book back in 1969. Since then a great deal of excellent history has been produced by the dozens of professional academics who study and teach the region's history. This book is based on their work. Many subjects were checked on the web, a quick and easy supplement to research in the secondary sources but no substitute for such books.

Much of the province's history can also be traced through the excellent entries in the Canadian Dictionary of Biography. Some of the more important ones researched for this project include William Annand, Hiram Blanchard, William Fielding, Philip Hill, Simon Holmes, Joseph Howe, James Johnston, Angus Macdonald, George Murray, John Parr, William Pipes, Edgar Rhodes, Charles Tupper, James Uniacke, John Wentworth, and William Young. The main secondary sources include:

Beck, J. Murray, Joseph Howe, Montreal, 1982.

—The Government of Nova Scotia, Toronto, 1957.

—The Politics of Nova Scotia, Toronto, 1985.

Bickerton, James, Nova Scotia and the Politics of Regional Development, Toronto, 1990.

Bruce, Harry, An Illustrated History of Nova Scotia, Halifax, 1997.

Conrad, Margaret, and J. Hiller, Atlantic Canada – A Region in the Making, Don Mills, 2001.

Dyck, Rand, Provincial Politics in Canada, Scarborough, 1986.

Fingard, Judith, Janet Guilford and David Sutherland, Halifax, The First 250 Years, Halifax, 1999.

Forbes, Ernest and D.A, Muise, ed., The Atlantic Provinces in Confederation, Toronto, 1993.

Forbes, Ernest, The Maritime Rights Movement, Montreal, 1979.

Henderson, T. Stephen, Angus L. Macdonald, Toronto, 2007.

McNutt, W.S., The Atlantic Provinces, Toronto, 1965.

Pryke, Kenneth G., Nova Scotia and Confederation, Toronto, 1979.

Stevens, Geoffrey, Stanfield, Toronto, 1973.

Warkentin, John, A Regional Geography of Canada, Scarborough, 2000.

Acadia, Acadians, 3, 4, 5, 6, 7, 8, 9, 10, 11, 12, 14, 18, 19, 20
Acadia College, University, 19
Africa, 14
Africville, 18
Agriculture, see farming
Alexander, Sir William, 3
America, Americans, 12, 13, 14, 28, 29
American Seafarer's International Union, SIU, 57
American War of Independence, 12
Amherst, 2, 38
Amherst, General Jeffrey, 10
Anglicans, Anglican Church, 11, 14, 18, 19, 21, 22, 36
Annand, William, 29, 32, 33, 34, 35
Annapolis Royal, River, Valley, 1, 2, 3, 4, 5, 6, 8, 11, 26, 35, 39, 57
Antigonish, Antigonish Highlands, 2, 11, 19
Antigonish Movement, 49
Appalachian Mountains, 1
Arichat, 11, 18
Armstrong, Ernest, 46
Armstrong, Lawrence, 6
Assembly, 8, 12, 14, 15, 20, 21, 22, 23, 30, 31
Atlantic, 1, 16, 17, 29, 35, 39, 43, 46, 53
Atlantic Development Board, 61
Atlantic Provinces Economic Council, 59
Atomic Energy of Canada (AECL), 63, 64
Bank of Nova Scotia, 18, 42
Baptists, 19, 22, 40
Bay of Fundy, 1, 2, 3, 4, 9, 13

Bedford Basin, 1
Bell Canada, 62
Blacks, 13, 18, 19
Blanchard, Jothan, 21
Blanchard, Hiram, 32
Bluenose, The, 41
Board of Transport Commissioners, 55
Boston, 6
Bras d'Or lakes, 1
Bridgewater, 35, 39, 53
Britain, see England
British Empire Steel Corporation (BESCO), 45, 46, 47, 50
Buchanan, John, 66
Cabot, John, Sebastian, 2
Campbell, Sir Colin, 21, 23
Campbell, William, 12
Canadian Fishermen and Fish Handlers' Union, CFFU, 56
Canadian National Railway, 46
Canadian Seamen's Union, CSU, 57
Canso, 1, 2, 3, 5, 6, 58
Cape Breton, 1, 2, 5, 7, 9, 10, 11, 14, 18, 19, 20, 34, 38, 45, 47, 49, 58, 61, 63, 65
Cape Breton Highlands National Park, 51, 61
Cartier, Jacques, 3
Catholic, Catholicism, 3, 5, 6, 12, 18, 19, 20, 22, 25, 36, 41, 50, 59, 60
Charlottetown, 27
Chebucto, Bay of, 7
Chester, 62
Cheticamp, 11, 18
Chignecto, Isthmus of, 1, 2, 3, 5, 7, 8, 11
Christianity, 3

Index

Chronicle, The, 29

Church of England, see Anglican

Clairtone Sound Corporation, 63

Cold War, 58

Collins, Enos, 15

Colonial Patriot, The, 21

Communists, 55, 56

Condon, William, 25

Connolly, Harold, 59

Conscription, 43

Conservatives, Conservative Party, 19, 23, 24, 25. 26, 27, 34, 35, 37, 39ff, 45, 46, 47, 49, 52, 54, 57, 59, 60, 61, 65, 66

Cooperative Commonwealth Federation, CCF, 52, 54, 61, 65

Cornwallis, Edward, 7, 9

Cumberland County, 8

Cunard, Samuel, 16, 17

Dartmouth, 18, 62

D'Aulnay, Menou, 4

Dalhousie, Governor, 16

Dalhousie University, 16, 19, 36, 50

Debert, 53

De Drucour, Chevalier, 10

De la Tour, Charles, 4

De Monts, Pierre du Guast, 3

DesBarres, Joseph Frederick Wallet, 14

Deutronium of Canada, Ltd, DCL, 63,64

Diefenbaker, John, 61, 64

Digby, 1, 35, 39

Dominion Coal Company, 38

Dominion Iron and Steel Company, 38

Dominion Steel and Coal Corporation, DOSCO, 50, 64

Drummond, Robert, 38

Du Chambon, Dupont, 6

Duncan, Sir Andrew, 47

Durham, Lord, Durham Report, 22, 23

Dutch, 13

Eastern Extension Railway, 35, 37, 38, 39

Edward Augustus, Prince, 15

Education, 14, 18, 19, 21, 26, 27, 28, 30, 36, 42, 60, 62, 65

England, English, 2, 3, 4, 5, 6, 7, 8, 9, 10, 11, 13, 14, 15, 16, 17, 18, 22, 23, 24, 30, 33, 43

English Harbour, 5

Erickson, Leif, 2

Europe, Europeans, 2, 3, 5, 12

Executive Council, 8, 12, 15, 20, 22, 23

Falkland, Lucius Bentinck, 23

Farming/Agriculture, 3, 15, 16, 17, 31, 41, 44, 45, 49, 56, 57

Fenians, 30

Fielding, William, 37, 38, 39, 66

Fishing, fishery, 1, 2, 3, 11, 15, 16, 17, 41, 42, 49, 56

Forestry, 15, 16, 17, 41, 42, 44, 45, 56, 57

Fort Beauséjour, 7, 8

France, French, 2, 3, 4, 5, 6, 7, 8, 9, 10, 11, 15, 43, 51

Fundy shore, see Bay of Fundy

Gabarus Bay, 5, 6, 10

General Electric of Canada, 64

General Mining Association, 17

Georgia, 1

Germans, Germany, 8, 13, 43, 52, 53, 54

Glace Bay, 47, 63

Grand Pré, 3,

Greenwood, 53

Grey, Earl, 24

Gulf of St. Lawrence, see St.
Lawrence
Haliburton, Thomas Chandler, 21
Halifax Explosion, 44
Halifax Catholic, The, 25
Halifax and Southwestern Railway,
39
Halifax Banking Company, 18
Hall, W.L., 46
Hants County, 8
Harrington, Gordon, 49, 50
Harvey, John, 24
Hicks, Henry, 59, 60, 61, 65
Hill, Phillip Cataret, 34, 35, 36
Holmes, Hugh, 35, 36
Howe, Joseph, 21, 22, 23, 24, 25, 26,
30, 31, 32, 33, 34
Île Royale, see Cape Breton
Île St.Jean, see Prince Edward Island
India, 5
Industrial Estates Limited, IEL, 62ff
Intercolonial Railway, 26, 33, 35, 36,
38, 39, 46
Inverness, 50, 57
Irish, Ireland, 7, 12, 13, 18, 19, 30,
51, 59
Isthmus of Chignecto, see Chignecto
Johnston, James, 23, 25
Kavanaugh, Lawrence, 20
Keith, Alexander, Keith's Brewery,
17, 54
Kentville, 1, 2
King, Mackenzie, 46, 47, 52, 54
King's College, 14, 19, 36
King's County, 8
Knights of Columbus, 41
Korean War, 58
Labour Party, 45
L'Acadie, see Acadia

Laurier, Sir Wilfrid, 39
Lawrence, Charles, 7, 8, 9
Legge, Francis, 12
Legislative Council, 22, 35, 40, 47
Liberals, Liberal Party, 19, 25, 26, 34,
37, 39ff, 45, 46, 50, 52, 54, 57,
59, 60, 65, 66
Liverpool, 11, 53
London, see England
London and Plymouth Company, 3
Longfellow, Henry Wadsworth, 9
Louis XV, 5
Louisiana, 9
Louisbourg, 1, 3, 5, 6, 7, 10, 11, 61
Lower Canada, 16, 22, 28
Loyalists, 11-13, 14, 15, 18, 62
Lunenburg, 1, 6, 53
Macdonald, Angus, L., 50ff, 65, 66
Macdonald, Sir John A., 32, 33, 34,
36, 39
MacDonnel, William, 27, 31
MacLachlan, J.B. 45, 46
MacMillan, A.S., 52, 54, 65
Maine, 16, 46
Maritime Rights Movement, 46-47
Maritime Telegraph and telephone
Company, 62
Masons, 41
Massachussets, 6
Mauger, Joshua, 12
Mechanics Institute, 21
Medicare, 62
Methodists, 19, 40
Michelin Tire Company, 62
Middleton, 35, 39
Mi'qmak, 2, 3, 6, 7, 8, 12, 15, 18, 19
Miller, Wiliam, 31
Minas Basin, 3, 4, 8, 11
Mining, 17, 26, 38, 45, 56, 57

Monck, Governor General, 27

Montagu-Dunk, George, Earl of Halifax, 7

Murray, George, 37, 39, 42, 43, 45, 46, 66

National Policy, 38

New Brunswick, 1, 3, 7, 8, 9, 13, 27, 28, 30, 32, 33

New England, New Englanders, 3, 4, 5, 6, 7, 8, 11, 12, 16, 17, 18, 28, 38

New France, 6, 8, 10, 11

New Glasgow, 2, 34, 35, 38

New Hampshire, 15

New Waterford, 47

Newfoundland, 1, 4, 11, 27, 30

Nicolson, Francis, 4

North Mountains, 2

North Sydney, 39

Northumberland coast, shore, 1, 2, 5, 8, 9, 11

Nova Scotia Central Railway, 35

Nova Scotia Philanthropic Society, 21

Nova Scotia Technological College, 42

Novascotian, The, 21, 29

Ontario, 28, 29, 32, 33, 55, 65

Orange Order, 41

Pacific Ocean, 28

Parr, John, 13

Pepperrell, William, 6

Phips, Sir William, 4

Pictou, 1, 11, 17, 18, 19, 26, 37, 38

Pipes, William, 37

Planters, 11, 18

Port Hawkesbury, 64

Port Royal, 3, 4, 5

Portland, Maine, 42

Presbyterians, 12, 18, 19, 25, 36, 40

Progressive Conservatives, see Conservatives

Prohibition, 40-41, 43, 48, 62

Protestants, Protestantism, 7, 8, 11, 12, 14, 18, 19, 20, 25, 40, 41

Prince Edward Island, PEI, 5, 9, 11, 27, 30

Pubnico, 3

Quebec, 10, 11, 28, 29, 32, 38, 43, 55, 65

Quebec City, 28

Railways, 17, 26, 35, 36, 37, 38, 41, 46, 47

Reciprocity Treaty, 26

Reformers, 21, 22, 23, 24, 25

Regan, Gerald, 65, 66

Reserve Mines, 47

Rhodes, Nelson, 46, 47, 48, 49

Saint John, 42

Saint Pierre and Miquelon, 11

Sam Slick, 21

Saskatchewan, 61

Scots, Scotland, 7, 12, 18, 19, 20, 51

Senate, 22, 28, 29

Seven Year's War, 6, 11

Sheet Harbour, 1

Shelburne, 1, 13, 53

Sherbroke, Sir John, 16

Shipping/Shipbuilding, 16, 18, 41, 53, 57

Shirley, William, 6

Shubenacadie Canal, 17

Smith, Ike, 64, 65, 66

Sobey, Frank, 62

Spevack, Jerome, 63, 64

Springhill, 2, 38

South Mountains, 2

Stanfield, Robert, 57ff

St. Croix River, 3

St. Francis Xavier University, 19, 50

St. George's Church, 15

St. John's Island, see Prince Edward Island

St. Lawrence Gulf, River, 3, 4, 5, 53

St. Mary's University, 19

St. Paul's Church, 7

Statute of Westminster, 32

Stellarton, 2, 63

Strait of Canso, 1, 2, 3, 4, 35, 37

Swiss, 8

Sydney, 14, 17, 18, 20, 38, 45, 53, 62

Temperance Society, 21

Thompson, Charles, 23

Thompson, John, 36

Tories, see Conservatives

Trade Union Act, 56

Treaty of Aix-la-Chapelle, 7

Treaty of Ghent, 17

Treaty of Paris, 10, 11, 13

Treaty of Ryswick, 4

Treaty of Utrecht, 4, 5

Trenton, 2

Truro, 1, 2, 18, 26, 42, 60, 62

Tupper, Charles, 26-32

Ulstermen, 12

Uniacke, J.B., 23, 25

United Farmers of Nova Scotia, 45

United Mine Workers, 46, 50

United States, 16, 17, 26, 30, 49

Upper Canada 16, 22, 28

United Church of Canada, 19

University of Halifax, 36

Vancouver, 46

Victoria, Queen, 15

Virginia, 4

War of 1812, 16, 17

War of Austrian Succession, 6

War of League of Augsburg, 4

War of Spanish Succession, 4

Wentworth, John 14, 15

West Indies, 5. 9, 16

Western Counties Railway, 35, 39

Whitney, Henry, 38

Williams, Sir Fenwick, 30, 31

Windsor, 2, 8, 14, 18, 19, 26

Winslow, Colonel John, 9

Wolfville, 2, 19

Wolvin, Roy, 45

Woman's Temperance Union, 40

Yarmouth, 1, 8, 11, 18, 35, 53

Young, William, 25